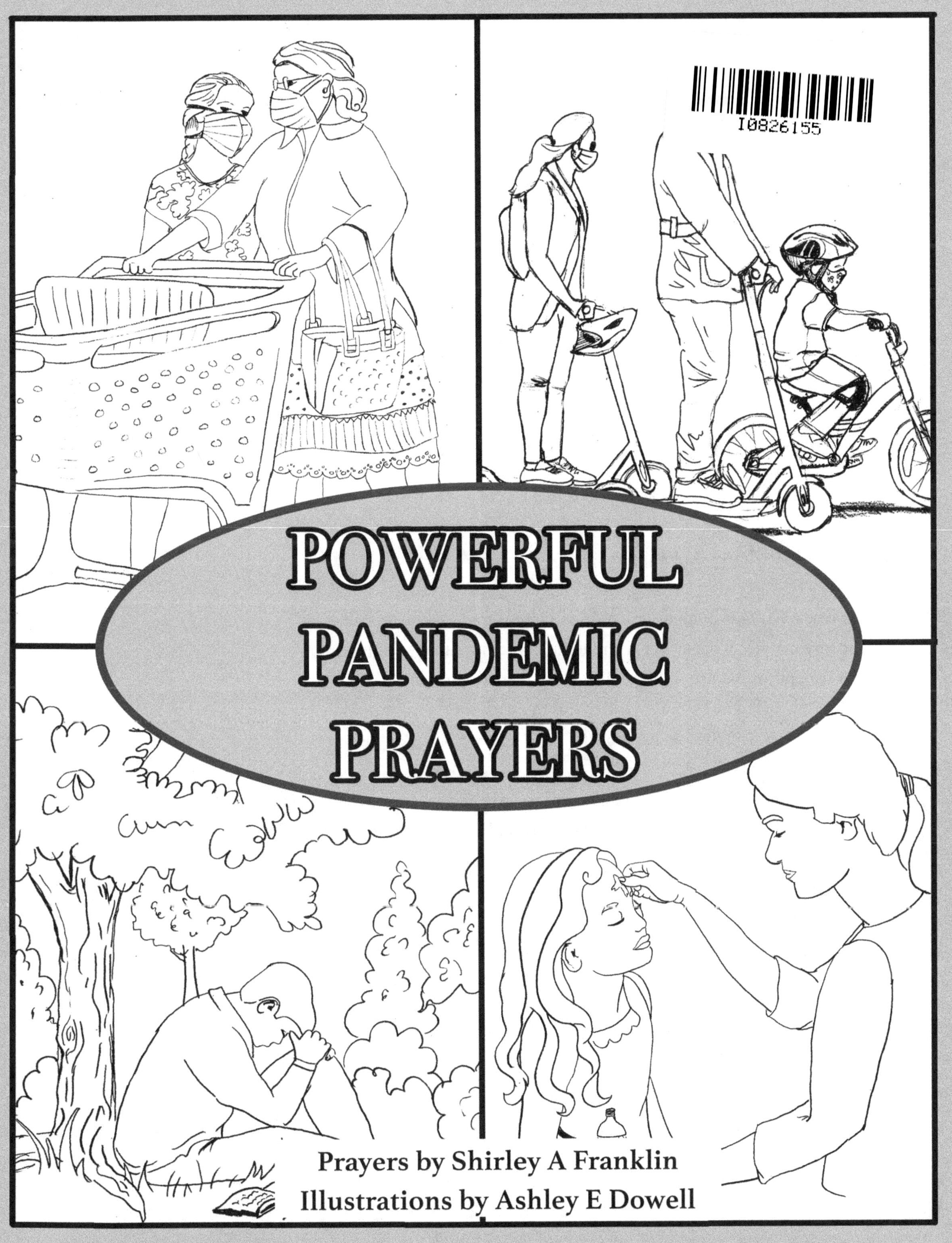

POWERFUL PANDEMIC PRAYERS

Prayers by Shirley A Franklin
Illustrations by Ashley E Dowell

ISBN-13: 978-0-9778520-2-4 (Paperback)

Any references to historical events, real people, or real places are used fictitiously.
Names, characters, and places are products of the author's and illustrator's imagination.

First printing edition, 2020.

Writezous Publishing
Ft. Worth, TX

Table of Contents

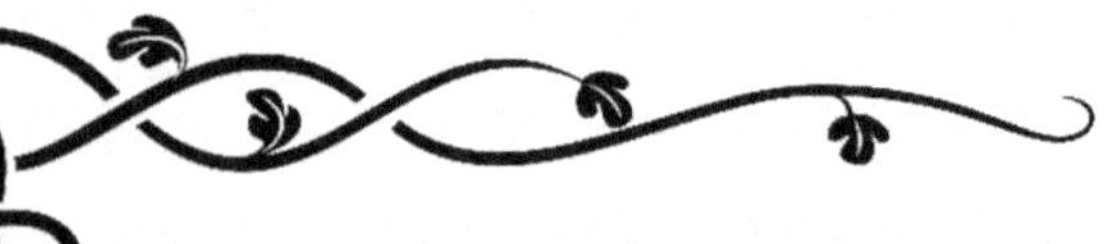

Invisible Adversary

Father, coronaviruses and other pandemics are invisible, but powerful. I pray that your greater power will come down now upon this earth, and bring an end to this challenging time of loss, limitations, and new ways of living under a threat that can't be seen, but is being felt all over the world. Heal the land, as only you can do. You are the invisible, yet invincible, omnipotent and omnipresent God. You have greater power than the coronavirus and other pandemics. Send that power now. In the name of Jesus, the divine Son of God.

Amen.

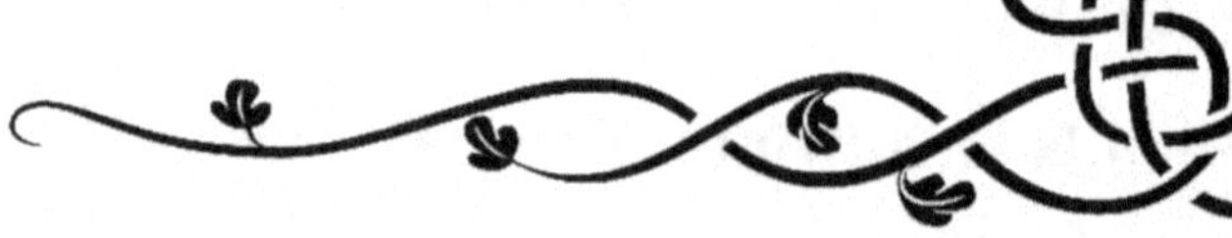

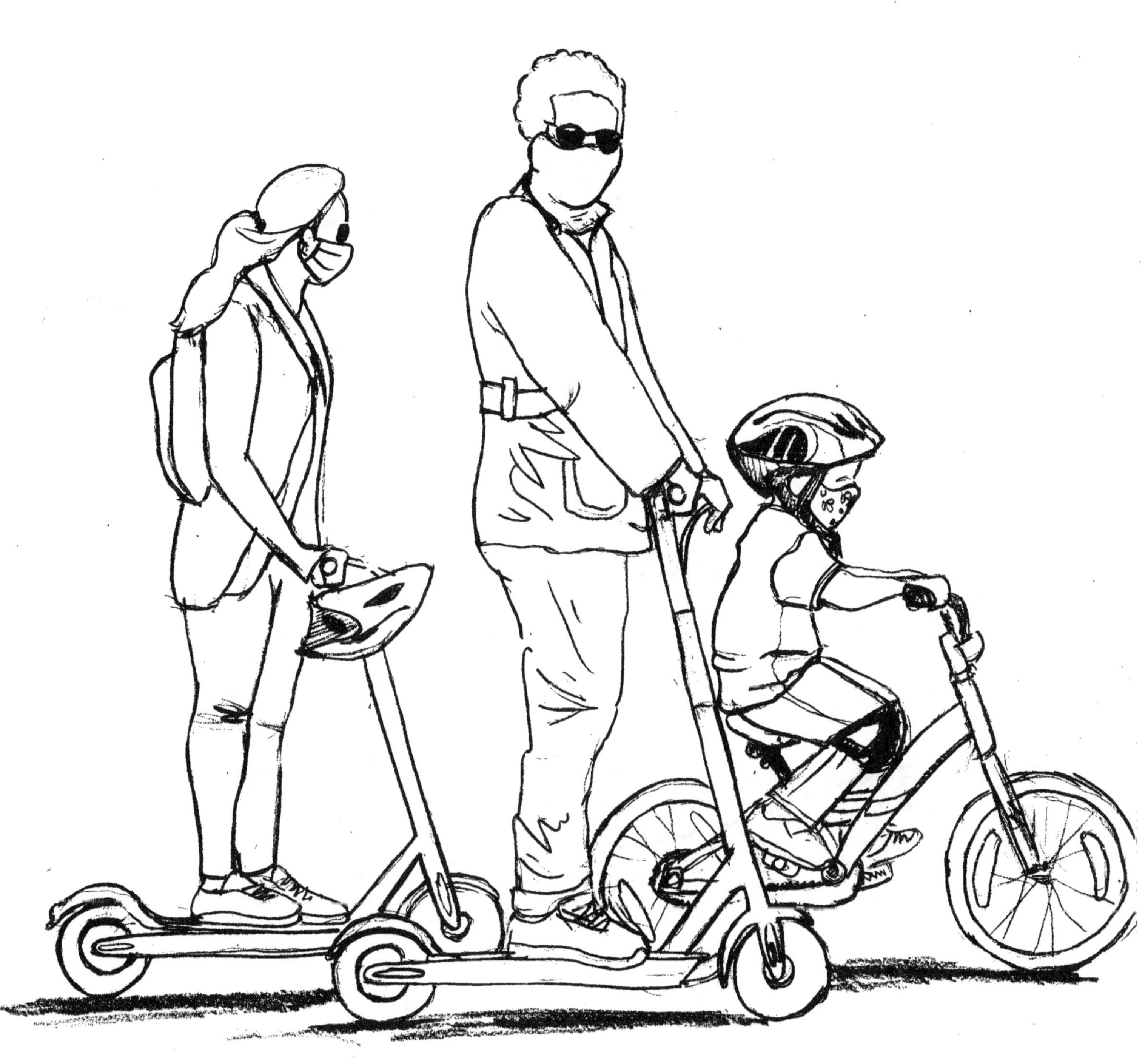

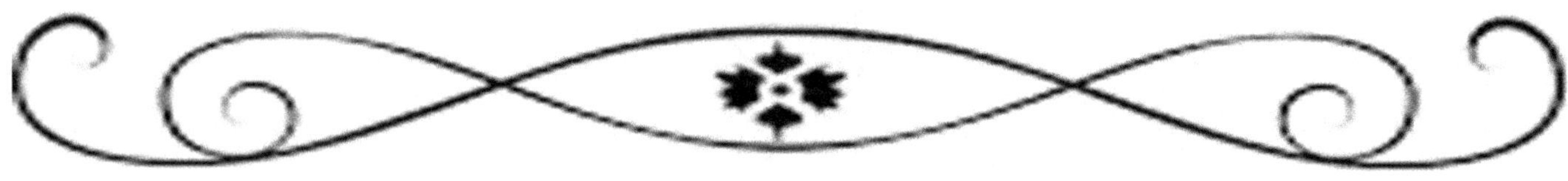

Undeniable Truth

God, you are the Master of Life.

You created me.

I'm asking you to preserve and sustain me during this pandemic.

Keep me safe from the contamination by the coronavirus and other pandemics.

In the name of Jesus, Emmanuel –God with us. Amen.

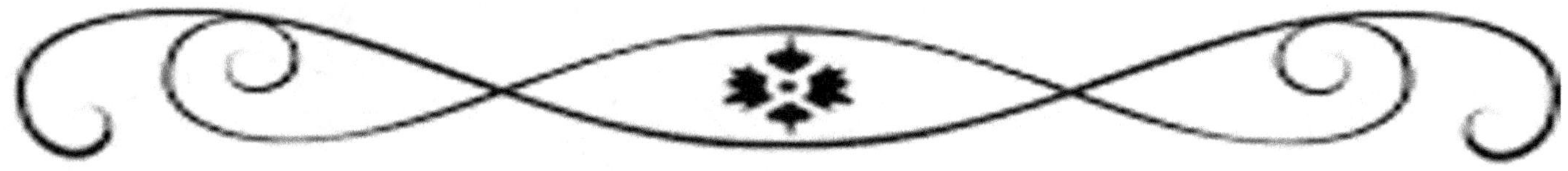

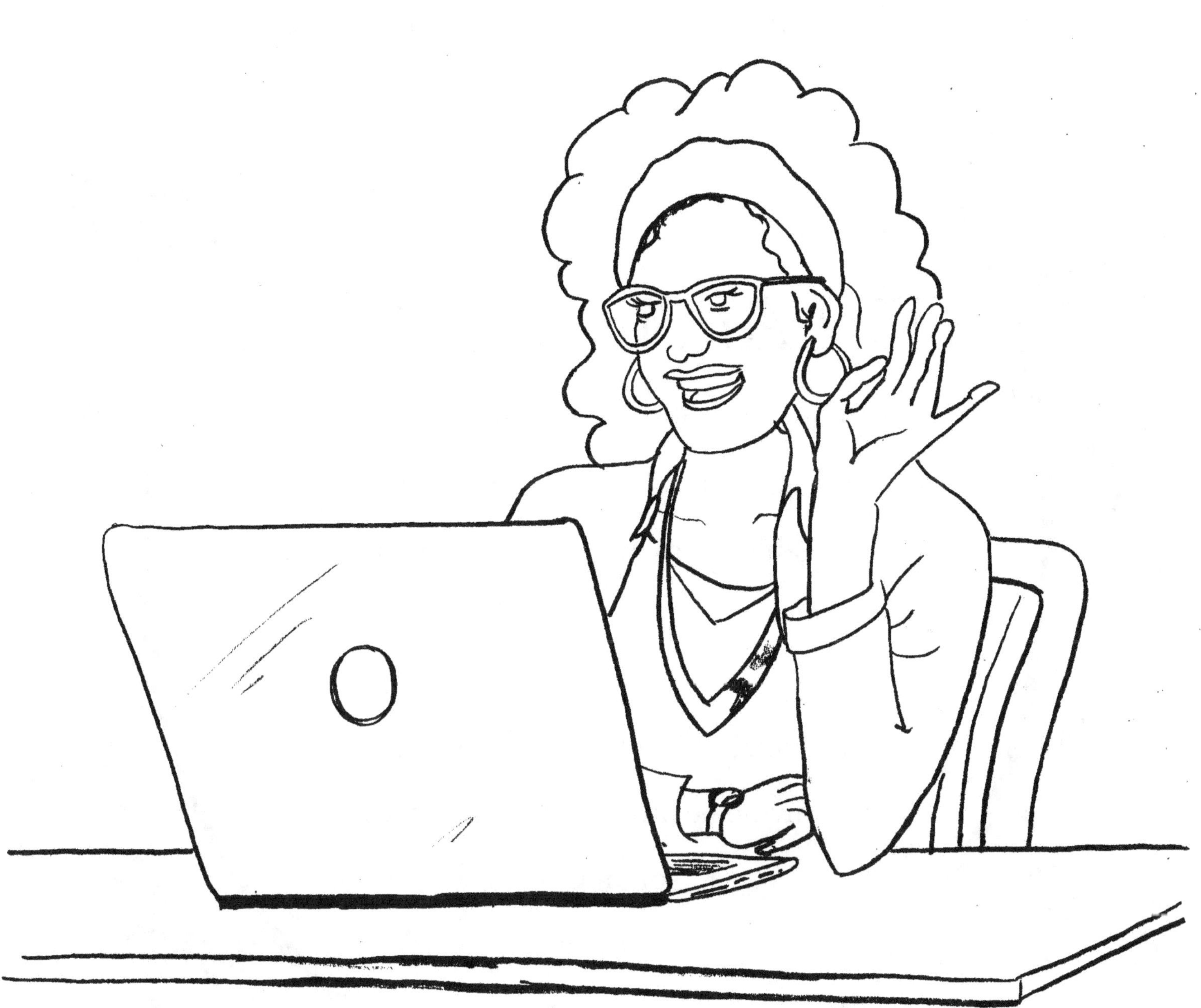

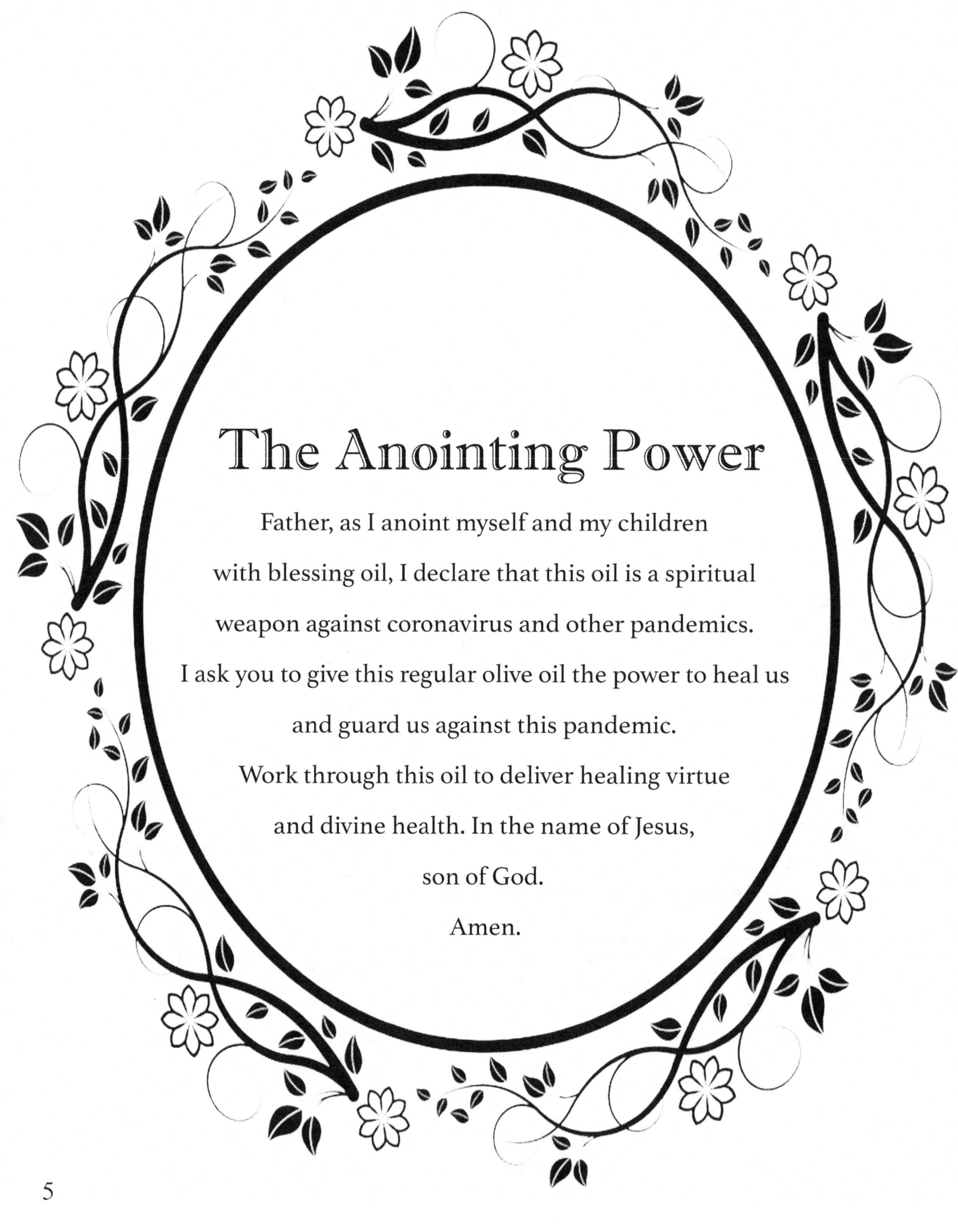

The Anointing Power

Father, as I anoint myself and my children
with blessing oil, I declare that this oil is a spiritual
weapon against coronavirus and other pandemics.
I ask you to give this regular olive oil the power to heal us
and guard us against this pandemic.
Work through this oil to deliver healing virtue
and divine health. In the name of Jesus,
son of God.
Amen.

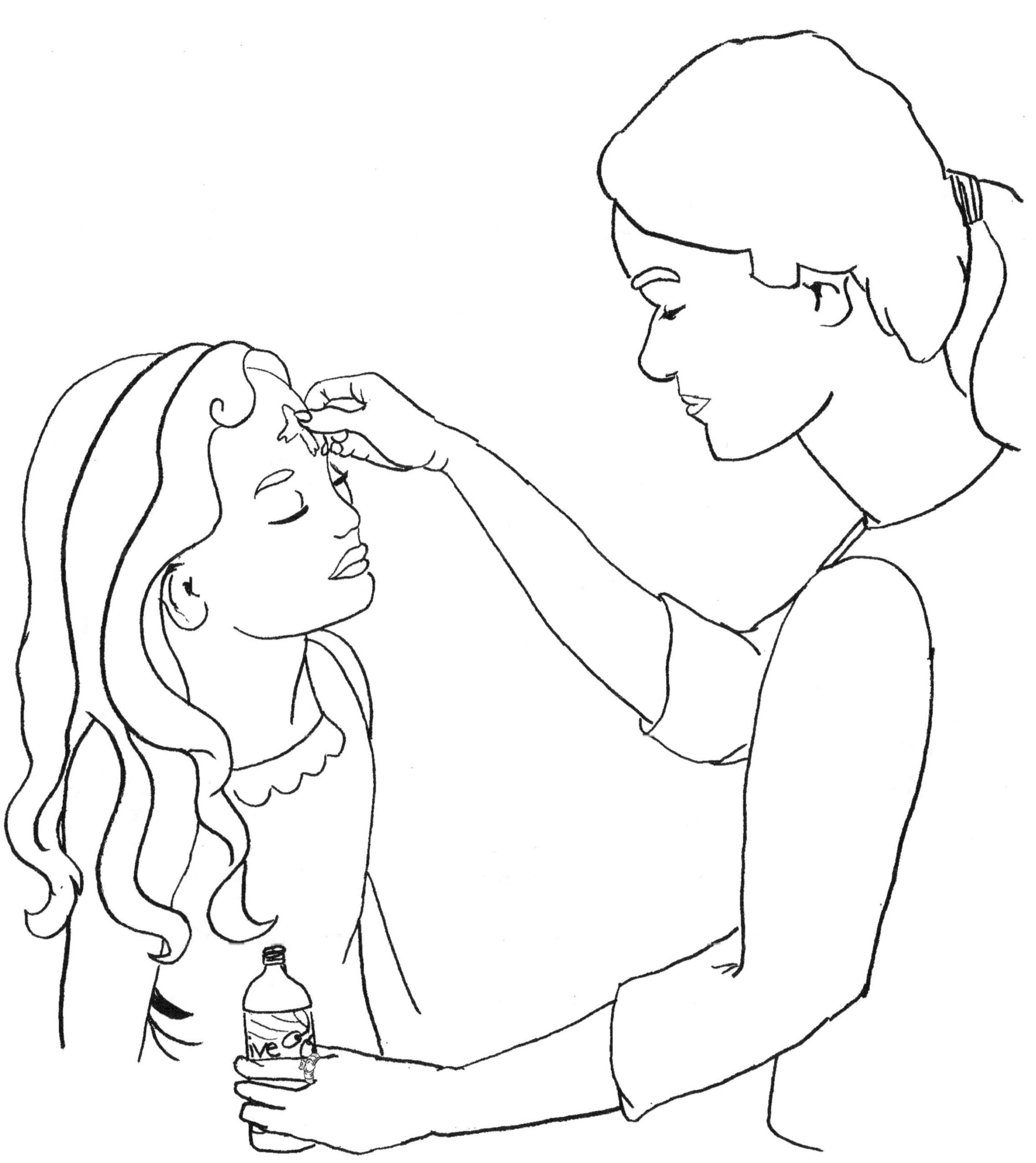

Fight for Me, Save My Children

Heavenly Father,

I'm asking you to fight for me

(in my job, in my home, at any place/situation

where someone is coming up against me),

and save my precious children

(from harm, defeat, sickness, pandemics and death).

In the name of Jesus, Son of Man.

I declare what Isaiah 49:25 says,

"For I will contend with him who contends with you,

and I will save (defend, preserve, rescue, deliver) your children."

In the name of Jesus, the one who so loves little children.

Amen.

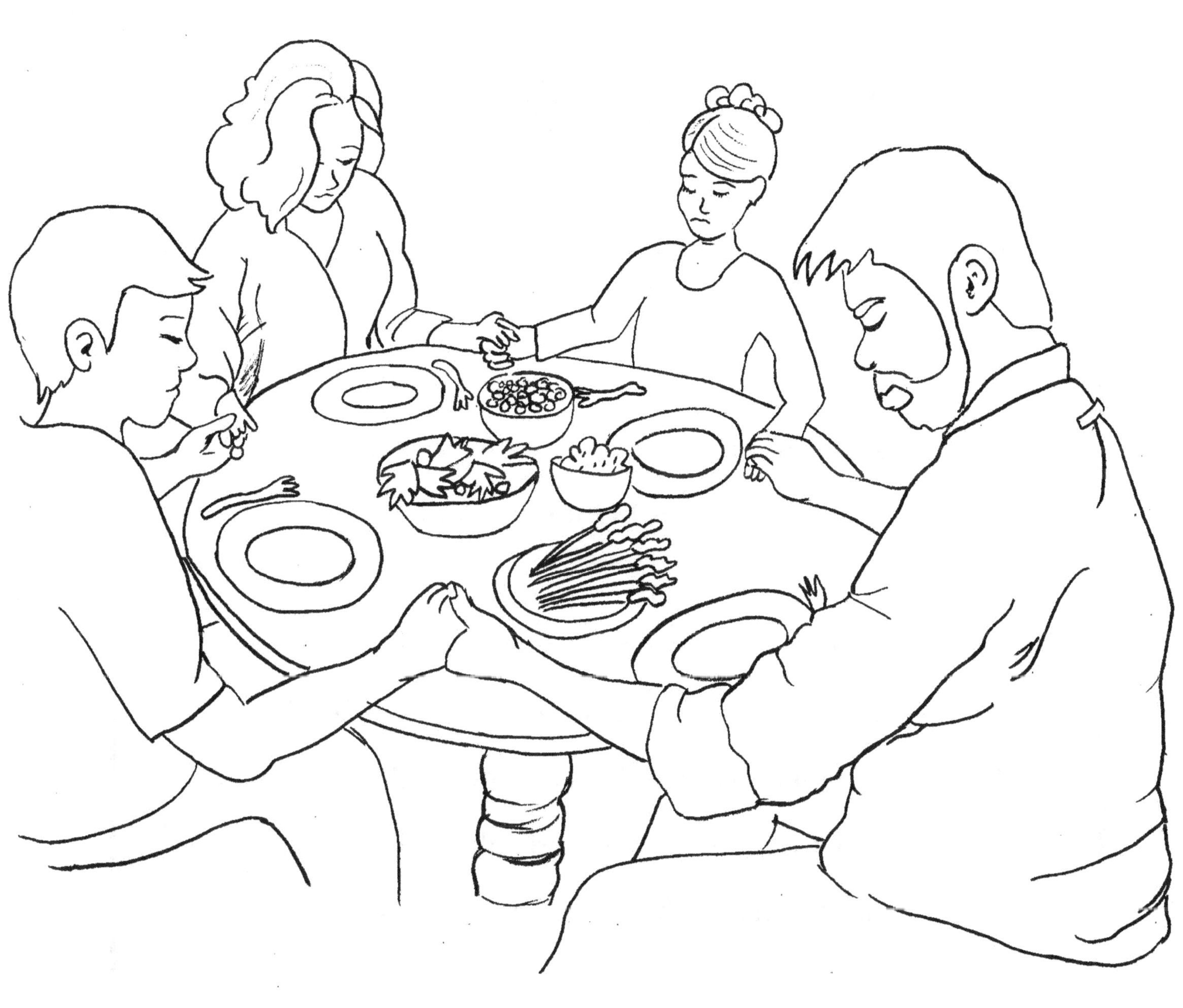

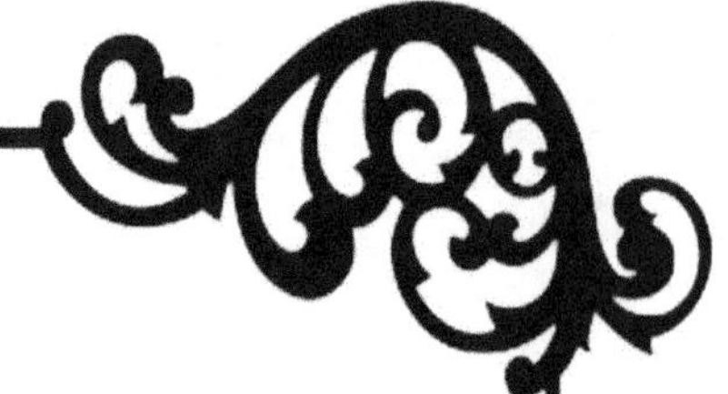

God Has Spoken

Father, I know that you repeatedly tell us that you have all power.

Psalm 62:11 says,

"God has spoken once, Twice I have heard this:

That power belongs to God."

I'm asking for your power to come down now,

and wipe this pandemic off the face of the earth.

Use your mighty power to drive out all pandemic viruses,

along with their damage and collateral effects,

and cast them into the abyss, the dry waste place.

In the name of Jesus, the Messiah. Amen.

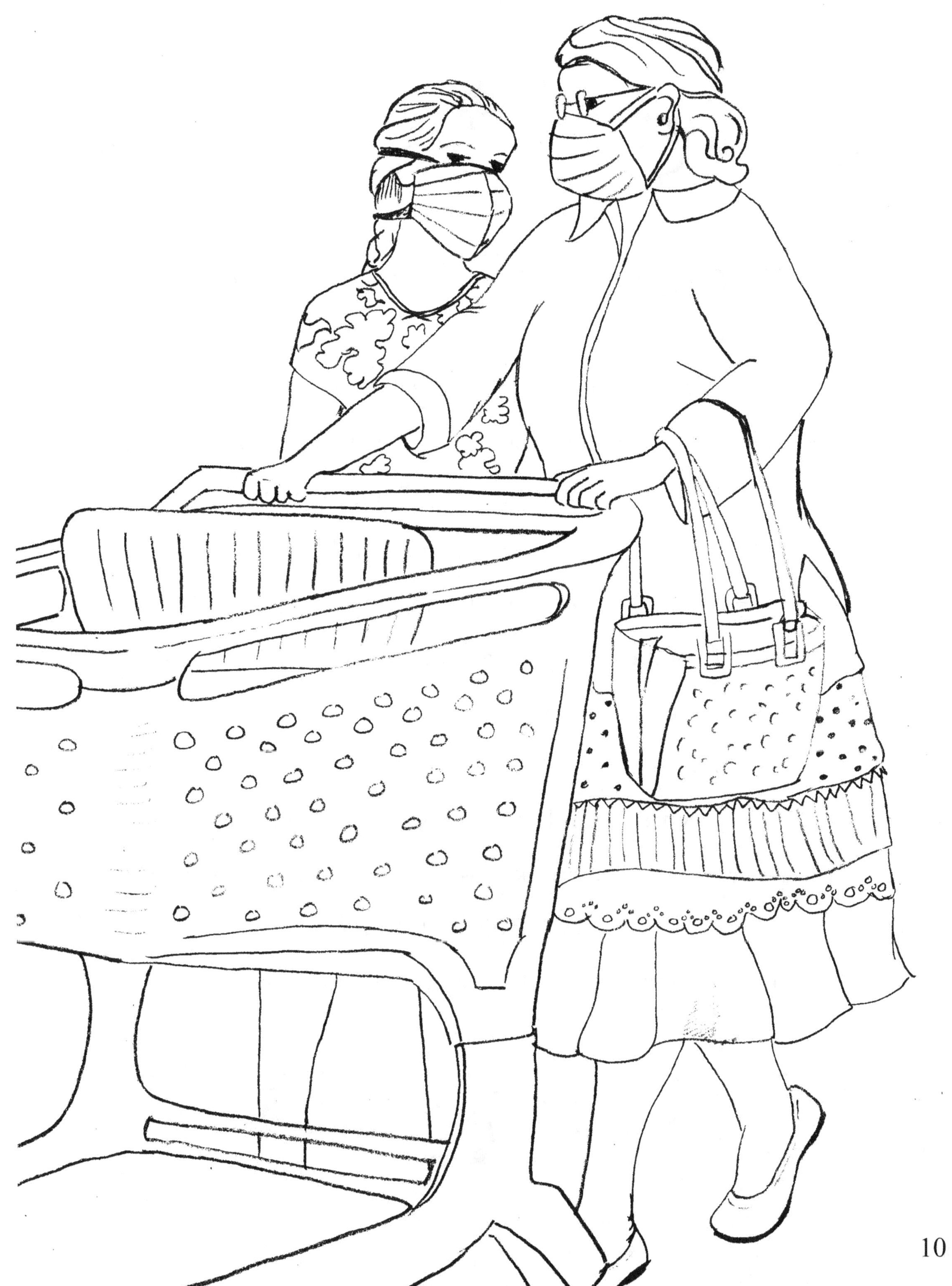

Salvation and Eternal Reward

Father, I'm standing in the gap right now.

My heart is concerned about those who are outside of your kingdom.

I pray that the lost today will hear the truth

from someone who is standing in Your divine presence,

and also standing in the gap.

The glorious truth of the Gospel of salvation has been hidden from the lost.

I pray that it will no longer be hidden, and that thousands,

and hundreds of thousands will hear the truth today,

receive you and confess you as their Savior.

I'm asking you to add partakers of the eternal reward of heaven

to your book of life today.

In the name of Jesus, the Captain of Salvation. Amen.

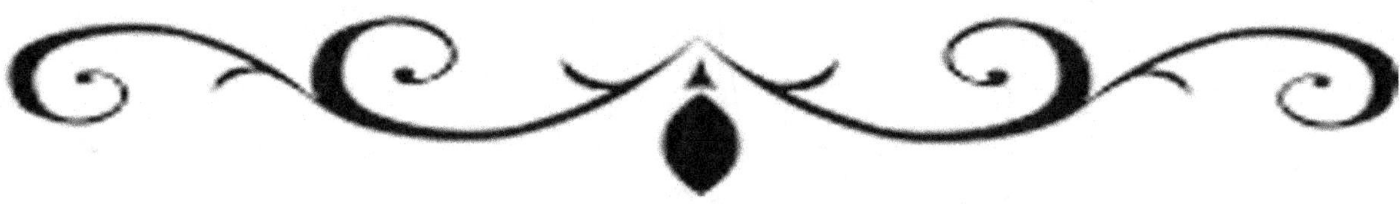

Find the way from Earth...

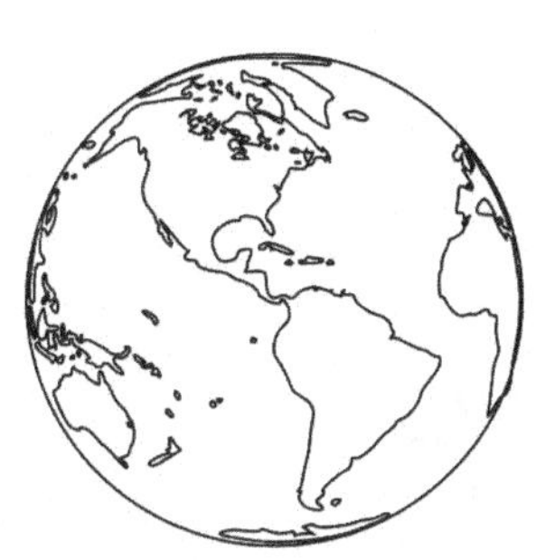

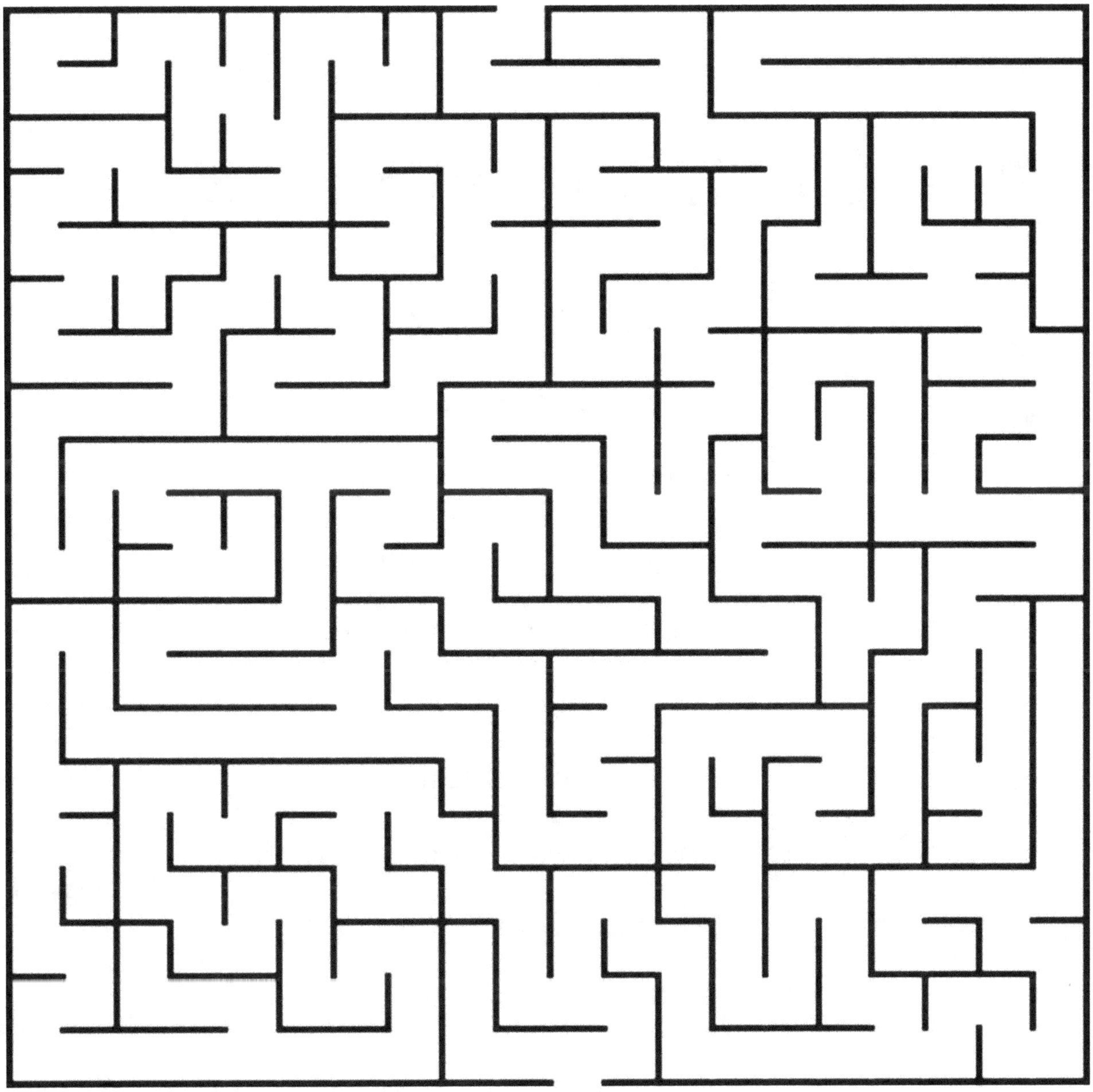

...to Heaven.

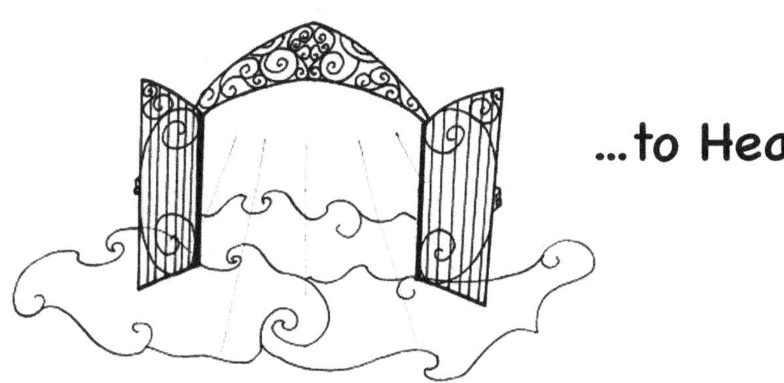

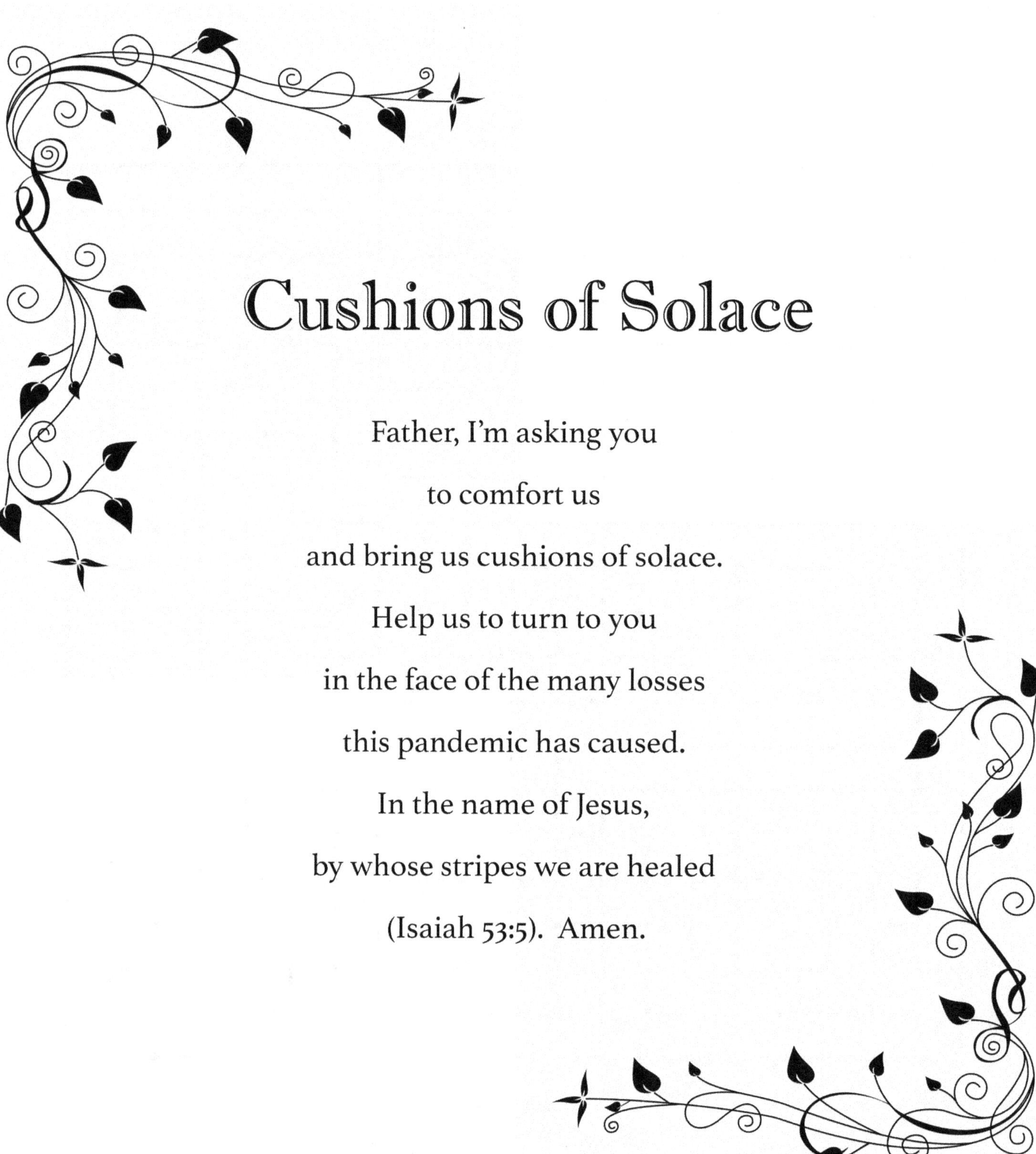

Cushions of Solace

Father, I'm asking you
to comfort us
and bring us cushions of solace.
Help us to turn to you
in the face of the many losses
this pandemic has caused.
In the name of Jesus,
by whose stripes we are healed
(Isaiah 53:5). Amen.

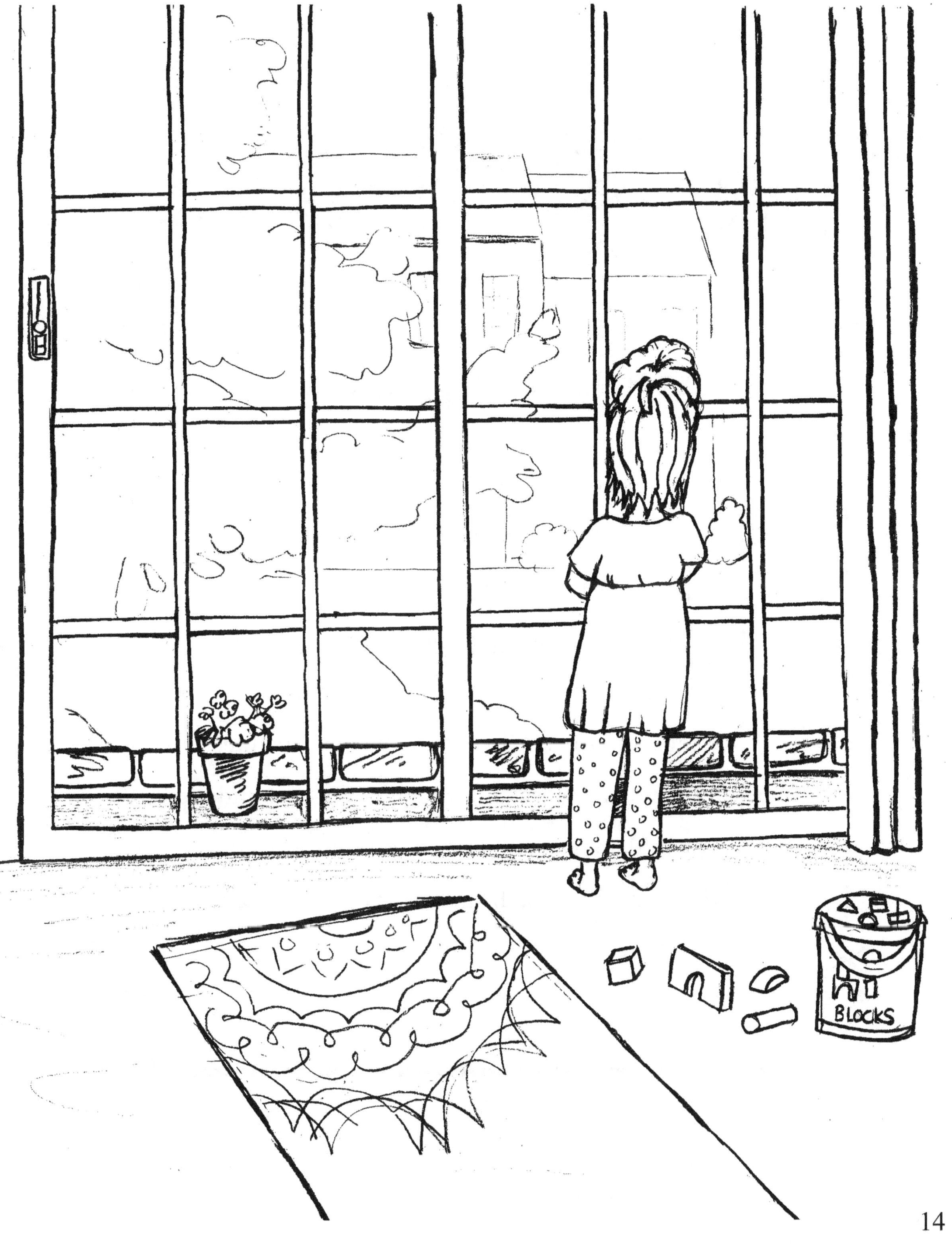
BLOCKS

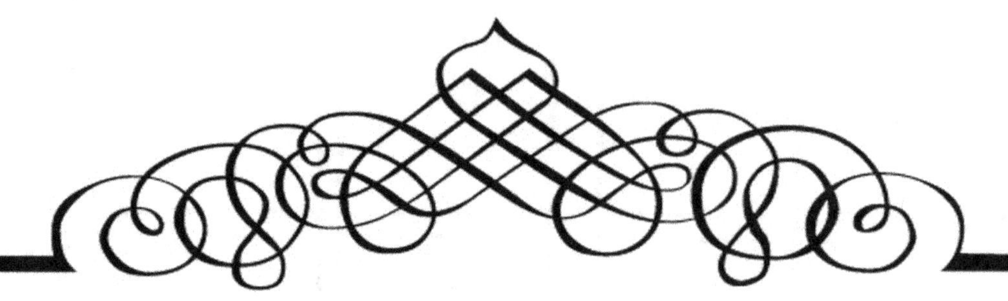

Abounding Cheer

Father, I know that you are always present with me.
I'm asking you to take away all of the sadness, grief,
depression and anxiety that this pandemic
has brought me – and give me abounding cheer.
Give me cheer, knowing that there are things that are going
well for me. Give me cheer and joy unspeakable,
in the face of this disease and what it's doing around the
world, in my country and community.
In the name of Jesus, the center of my joy. Amen.

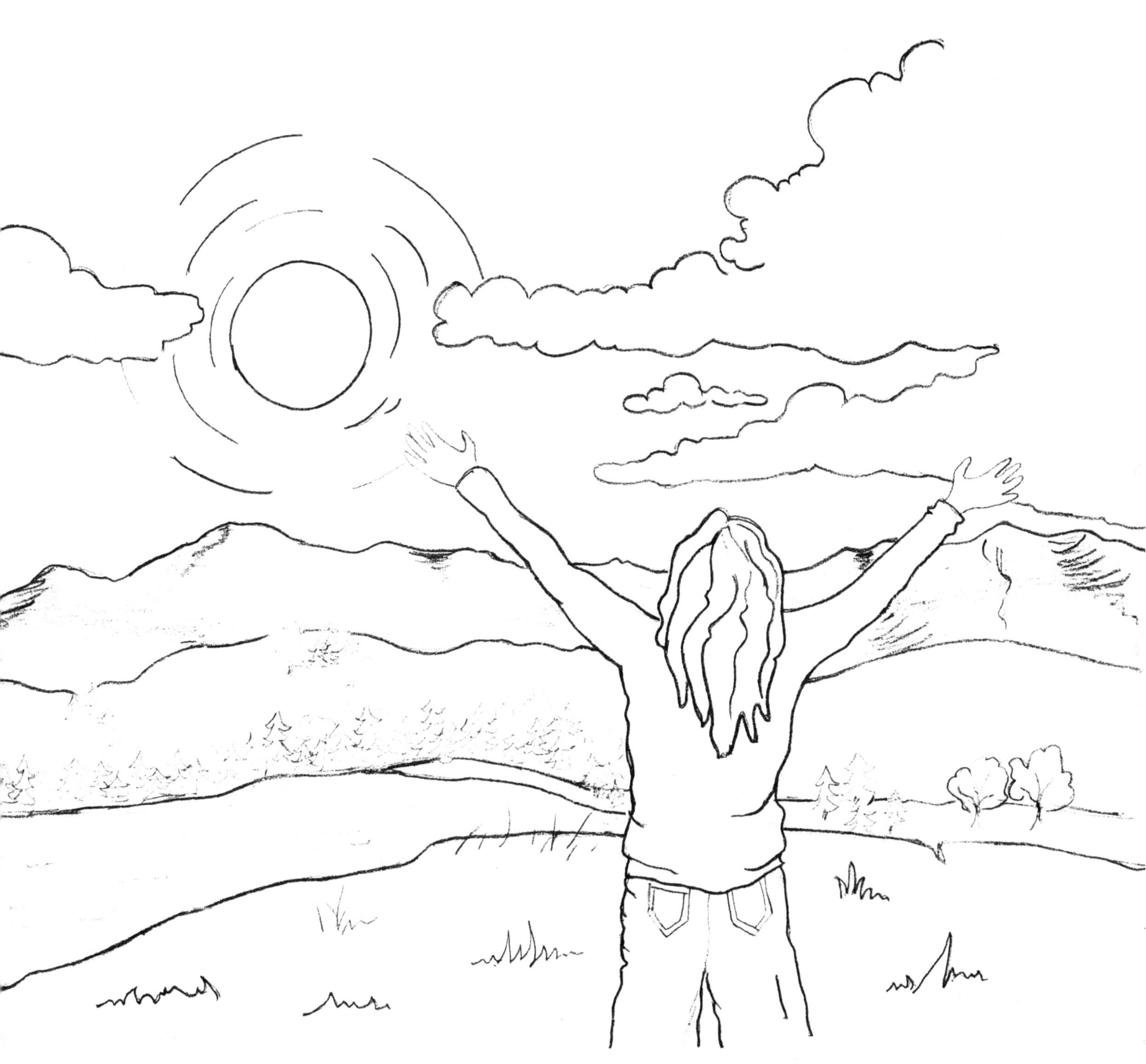

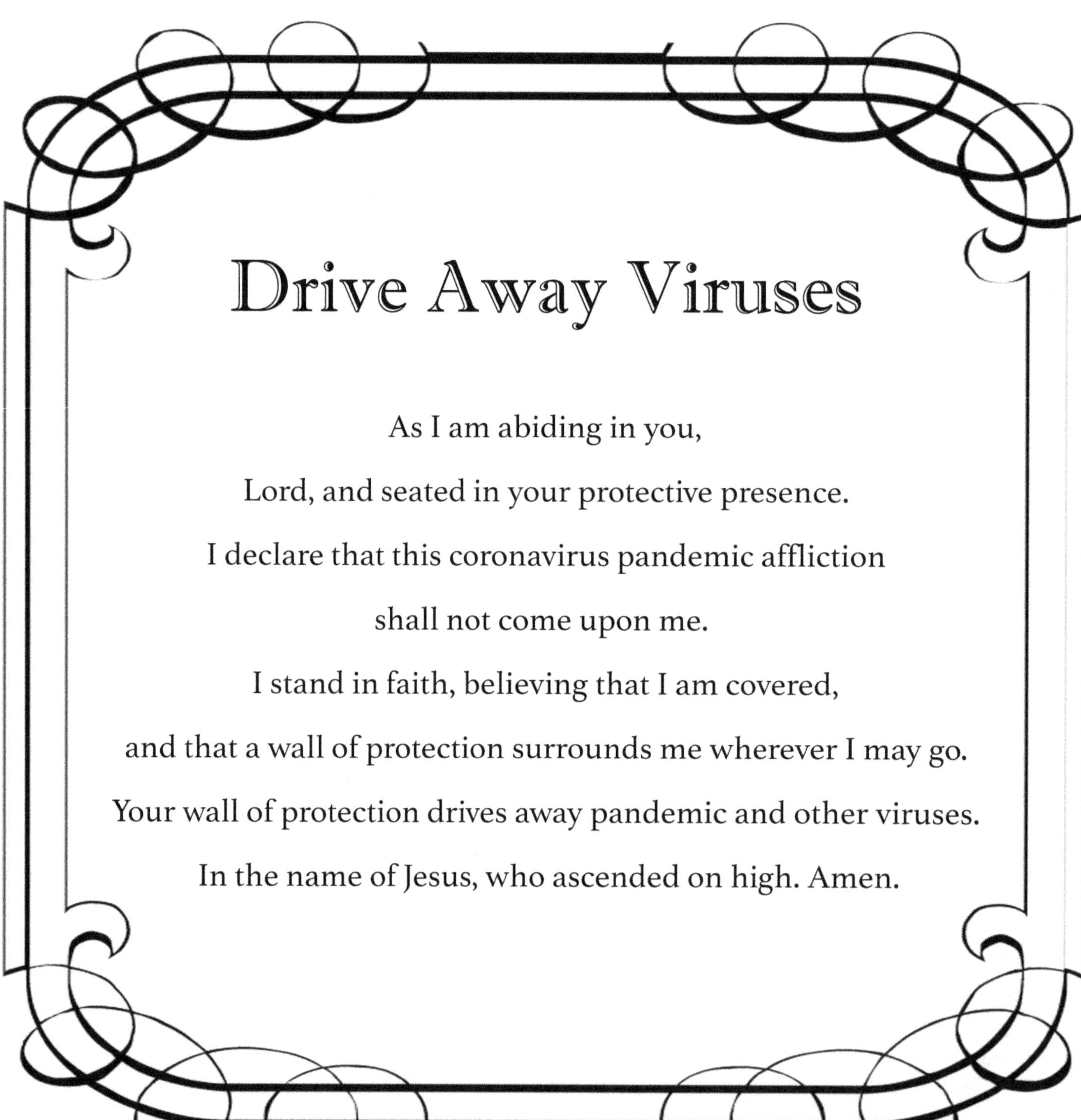

Drive Away Viruses

As I am abiding in you,
Lord, and seated in your protective presence.
I declare that this coronavirus pandemic affliction
shall not come upon me.
I stand in faith, believing that I am covered,
and that a wall of protection surrounds me wherever I may go.
Your wall of protection drives away pandemic and other viruses.
In the name of Jesus, who ascended on high. Amen.

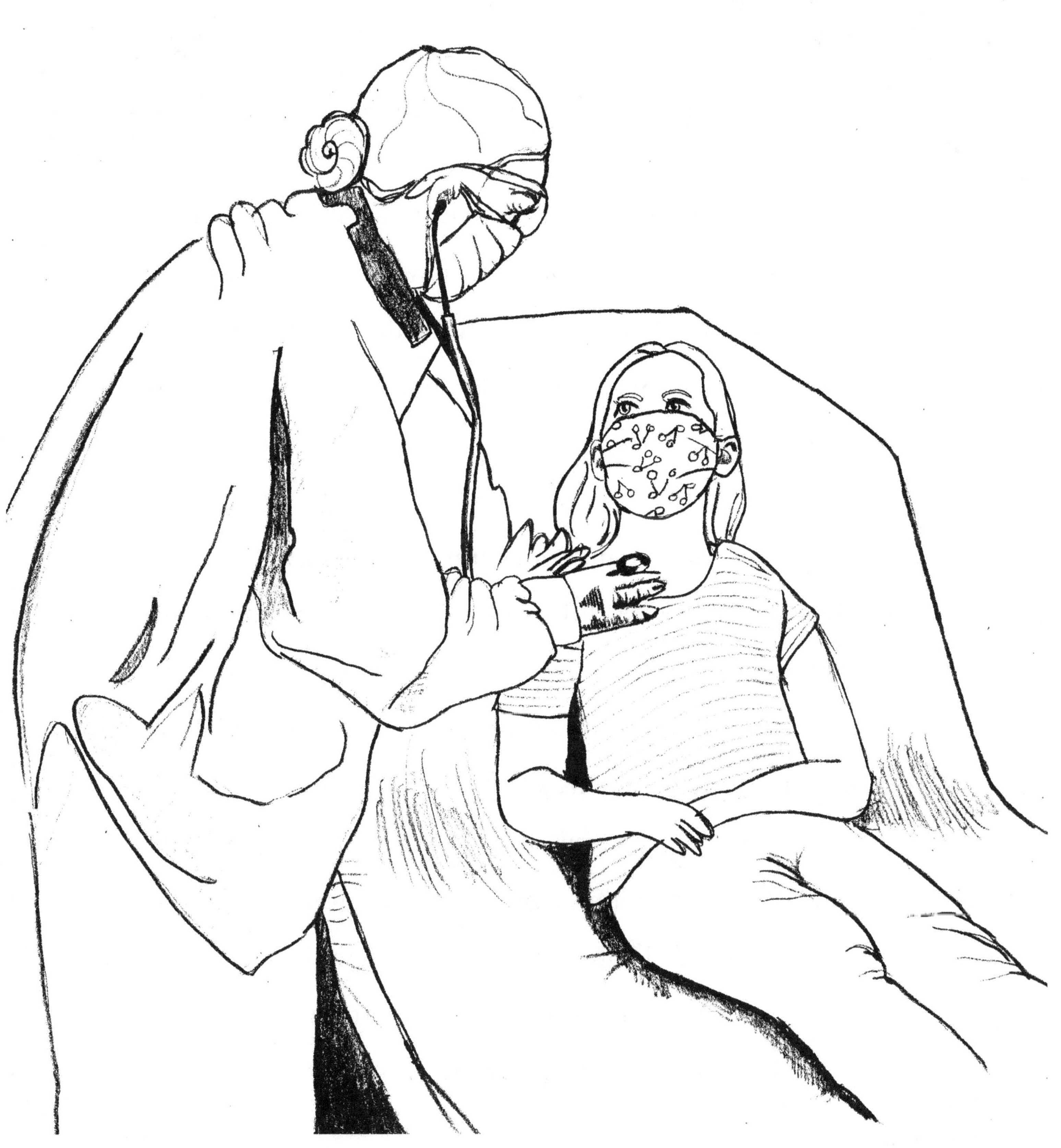

Word Weapon

Father, I pick up the Sword, your Word to defeat this pandemic and any others. Your Word has great power, and nullifies coronavirus and other pandemics. I stand on your Word.

I use the Sword of the Spirit, God's Holy Word, and I use it against all the forces of evil that are trying to diminish or take my life.

You said in Acts 3:19,

"So repent [change your inner self-your old way of thinking, regret past sin] and return [to God-seek His purpose for your life], so that your sins may be wiped away [blotted out, completely erased], so that times of refreshing may come from the presence of the Lord [restoring you like a cool wind on a hot day];"

In the name of Jesus, the Alpha and Omega.

So Father, I'm truly sorry for my sins. I turn away from the world's way. I come to you, on bended knee, crying out to you for forgiveness, help, mercy and restoration. I thank you that this prayer is answered.

In the name of Jesus, My Advocate. Amen.

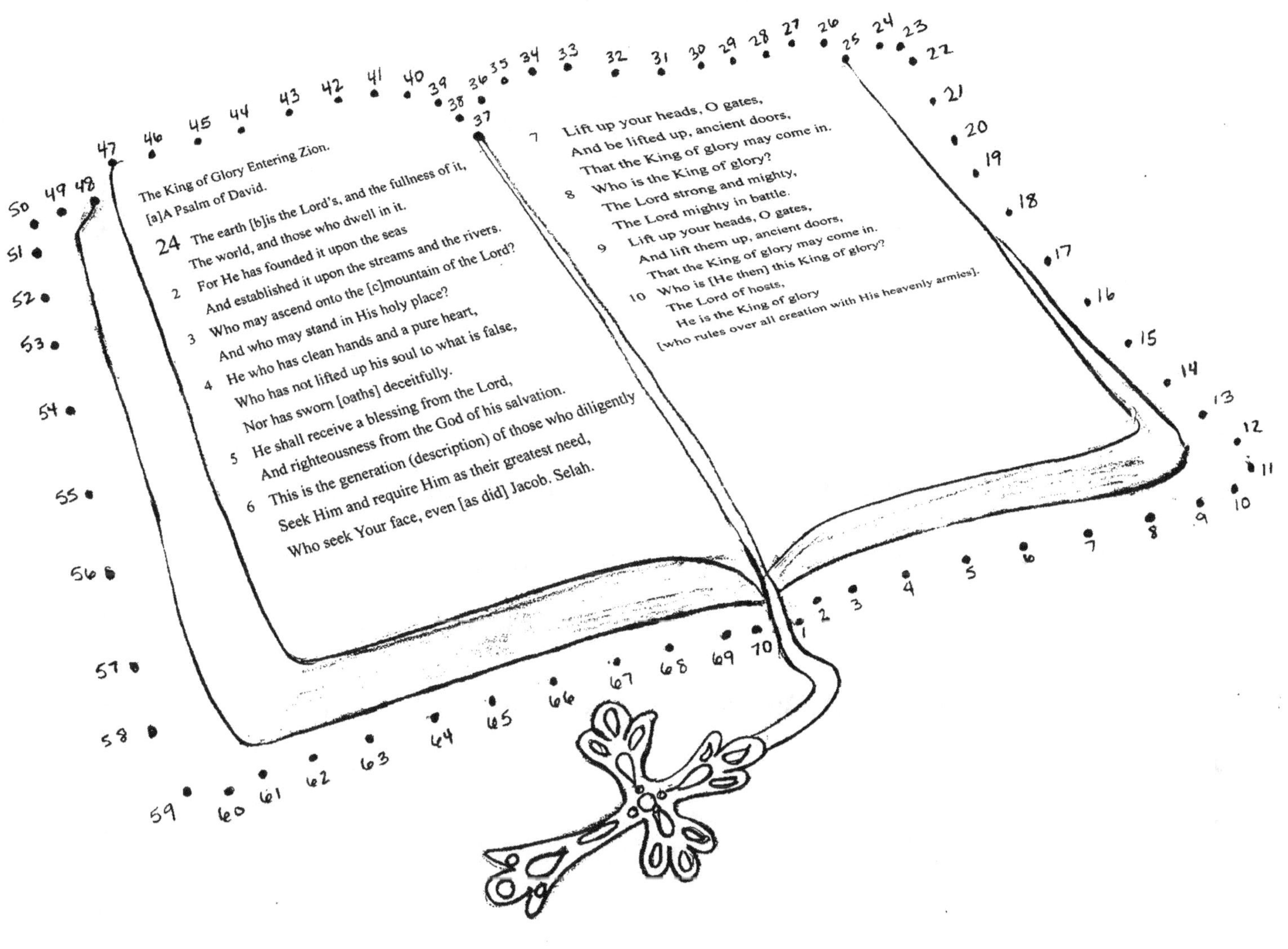
The King of Glory Entering Zion.
[a]A Psalm of David.
24 The earth [b]is the Lord's, and the fullness of it,
The world, and those who dwell in it.
2 For He has founded it upon the seas
And established it upon the streams and the rivers.
3 Who may ascend onto the [c]mountain of the Lord?
And who may stand in His holy place?
4 He who has clean hands and a pure heart,
He who has not lifted up his soul to what is false,
Nor has sworn [oaths] deceitfully.
5 He shall receive a blessing from the Lord,
And righteousness from the God of his salvation.
6 This is the generation (description) of those who diligently
Seek Him and require Him as their greatest need,
Who seek Your face, even [as did] Jacob. Selah.
7 Lift up your heads, O gates,
And be lifted up, ancient doors,
That the King of glory may come in.
8 Who is the King of glory?
The Lord strong and mighty,
The Lord mighty in battle.
9 Lift up your heads, O gates,
And lift them up, ancient doors,
That the King of glory may come in.
10 Who is [He then] this King of glory?
The Lord of hosts,
He is the King of glory
[who rules over all creation with His heavenly armies].

Weapons of Prayer and Faith

Heavenly Father,

I use my faith and prayer to defeat
the coronavirus and any pandemic,
affliction, disease, infirmity and sickness.
I ask you to not let them touch me or my family members,
loved ones, work associates and others in my circle.

In the name of Jesus, The Bread of Life.

Amen.

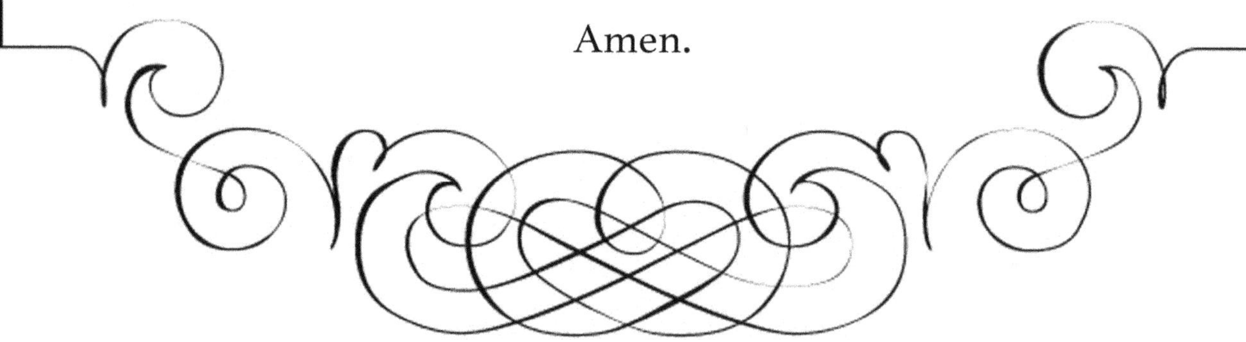

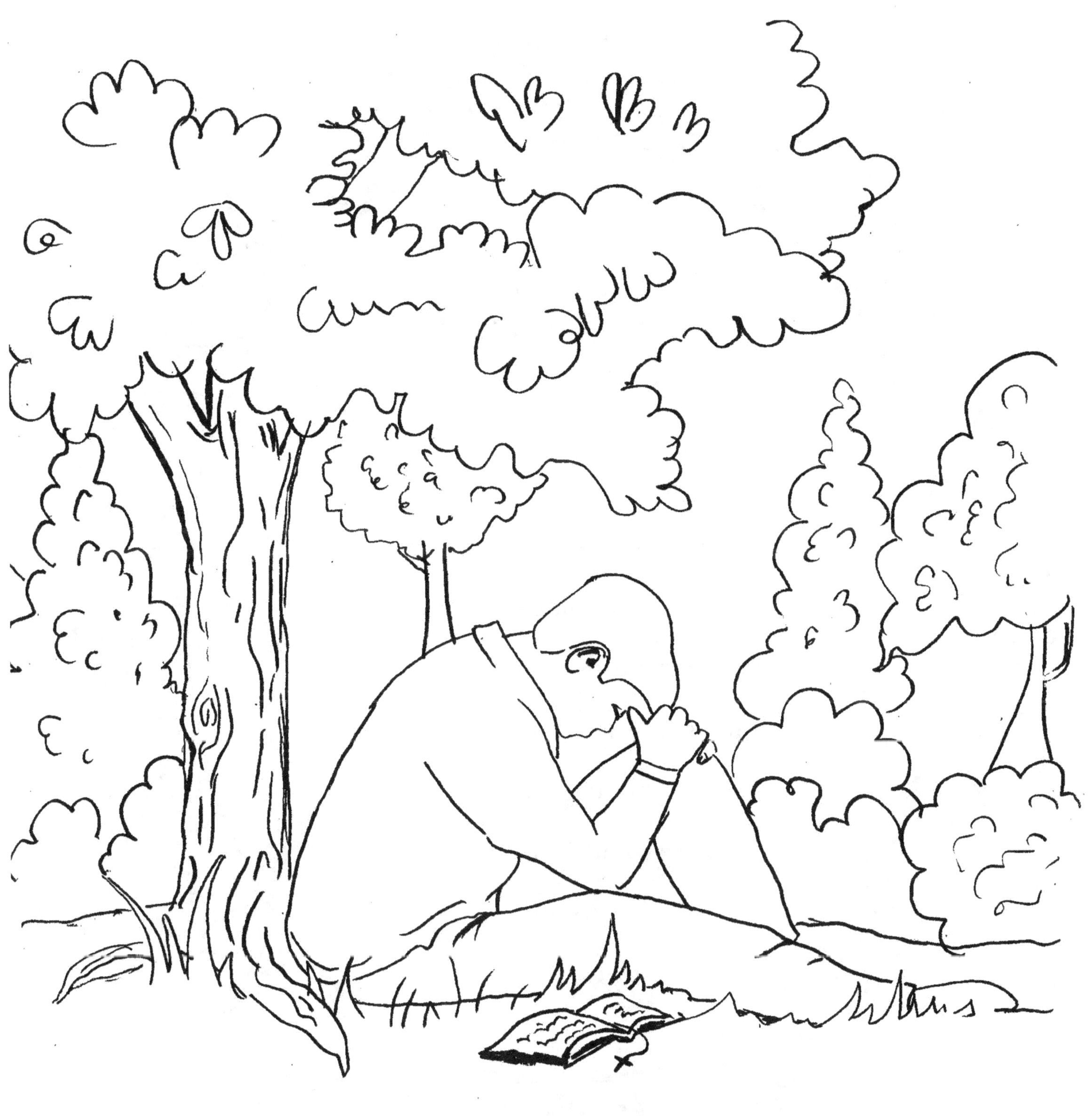

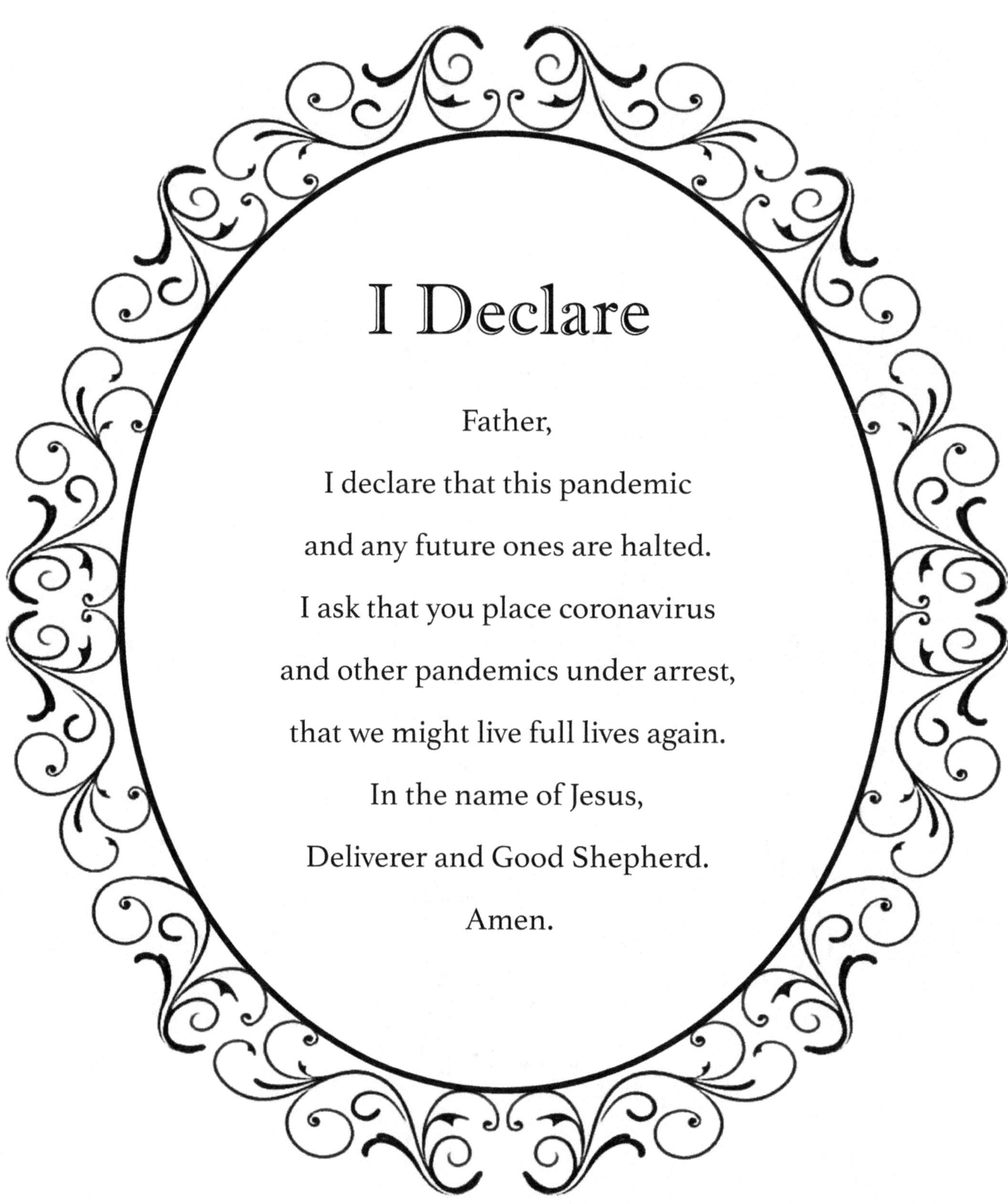

I Declare

Father,

I declare that this pandemic

and any future ones are halted.

I ask that you place coronavirus

and other pandemics under arrest,

that we might live full lives again.

In the name of Jesus,

Deliverer and Good Shepherd.

Amen.

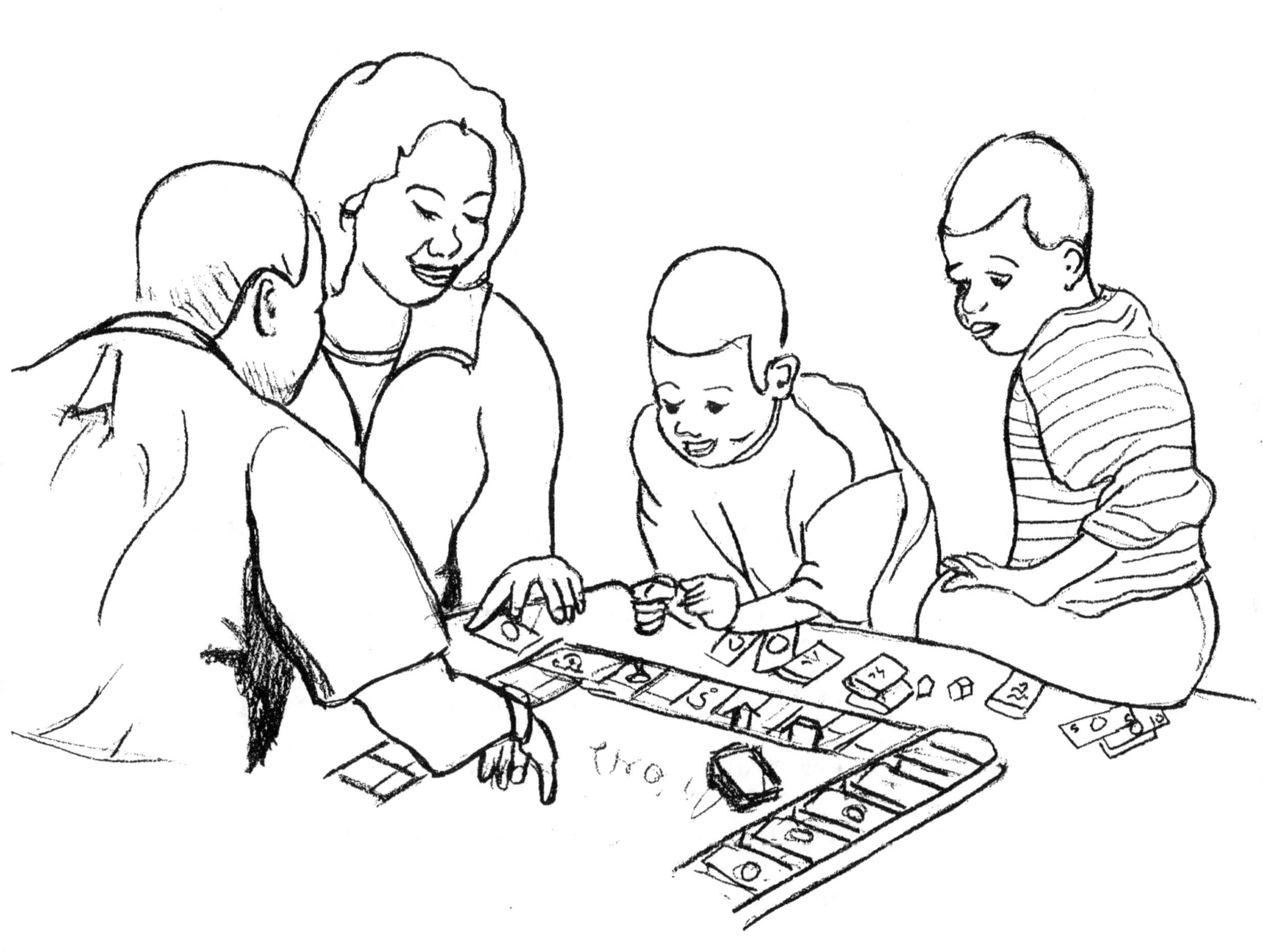

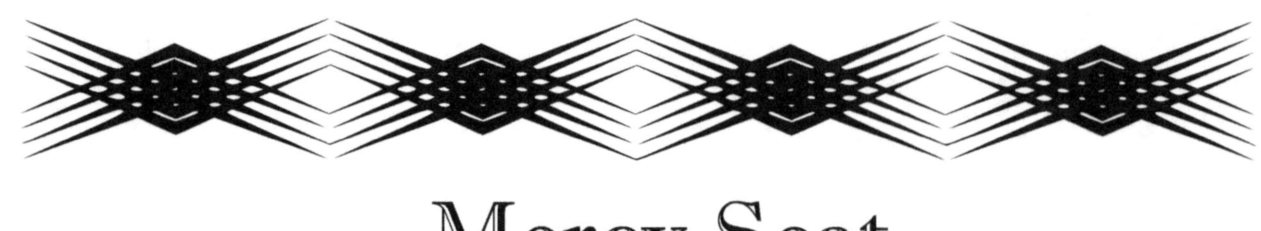

Mercy Seat

Lord God of Heaven and ruler of all the earth,

I come to your mercy seat. I'm asking you, Lord Jesus, to hear my prayer.

Father, hide me from this pestilence and other pandemics

that might arise in my lifetime.

Shield me from being contaminated.

Psalm 91: 3 says,

"For He will save you from the trap of the fowler. And from deadly pestilence.

He will cover you and completely protect you with His pinions,

And under His wings you will find refuge; His faithfulness is a shield and a wall."

Lord, I need you to raise that wall around me as

I venture to work and/or any other places where I go.

Protect me from contamination and contagion on every side,

from my head to my very toes. I need your new mercies every day.

Please grant them to me. In the name of Jesus, Faithful and True.

Amen.

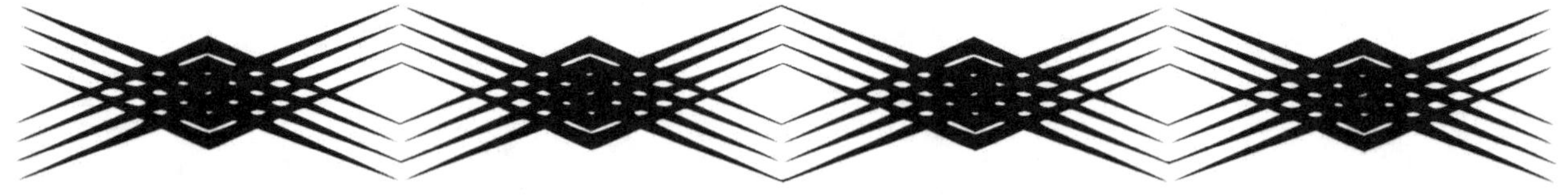

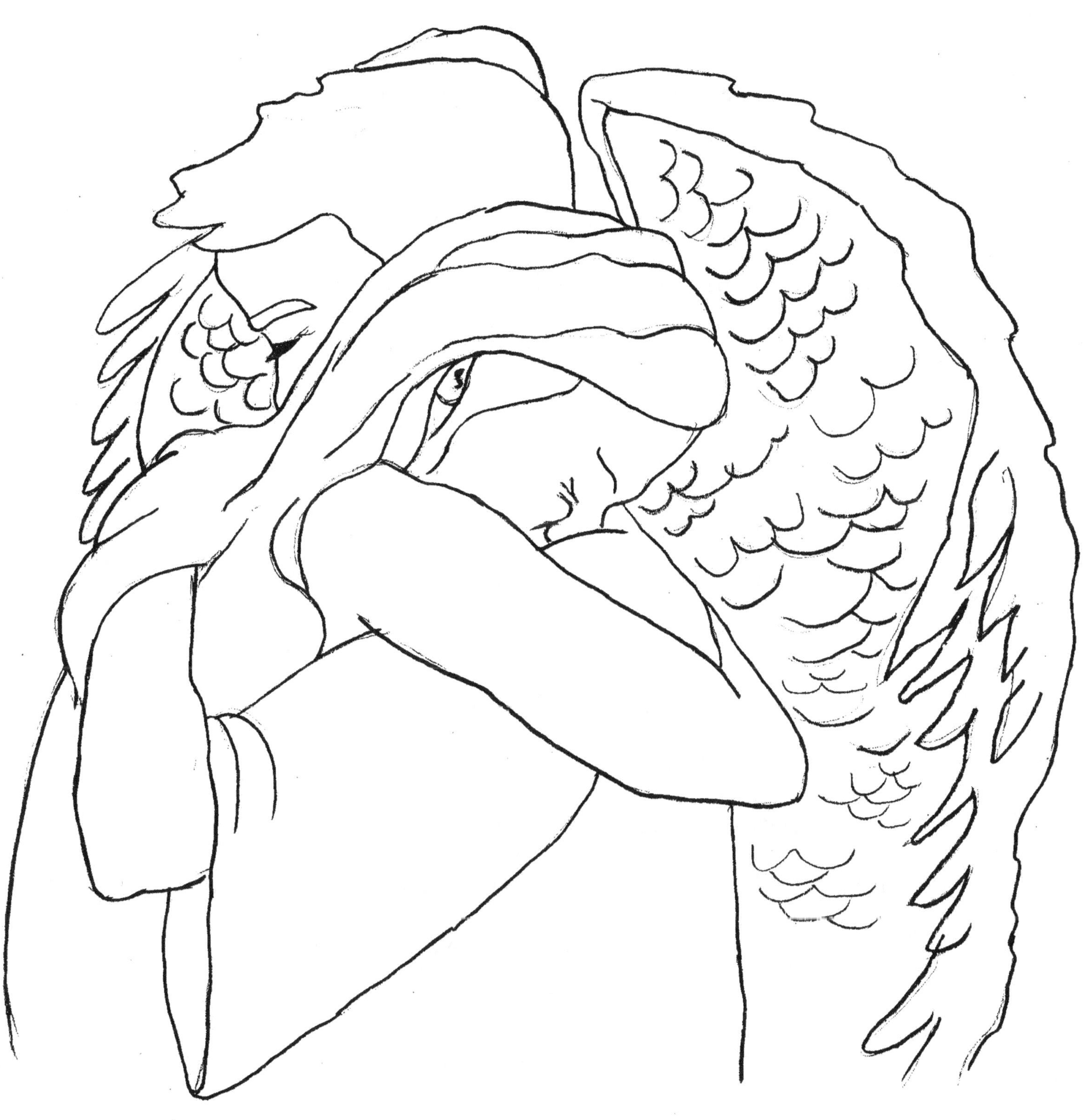

Disarmed by Jesus

Coronavirus, be scattered to the far winds.

Be dried up and vanquished from the face of the earth.

You have been disarmed by Jesus.

In Colossians 2:15, it declares,

"When He had disarmed the rulers and authorities

[those supernatural forces of evil operating against us],

He made a public example of them

[exhibiting them as captives in triumphal procession]

having triumphed over them through the cross."

Father, I stand firm in faith that

this pandemic and others were already defeated.

I declare that the manifestation of this disease's defeat

will present itself now all over the land.

In Jesus, The Resurrected Prince of Life's (Acts 3:15),

mighty name we pray.

Amen.

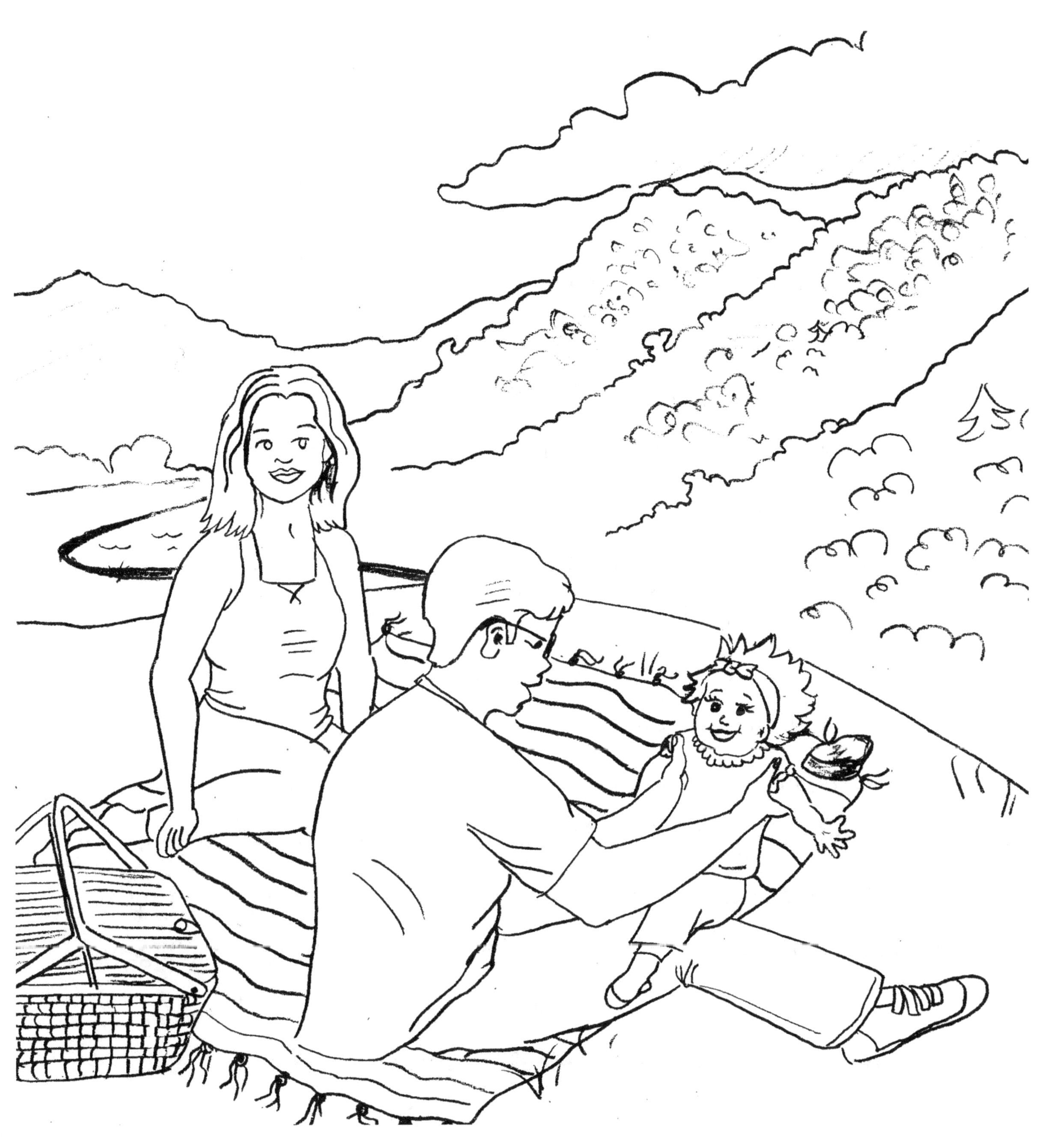

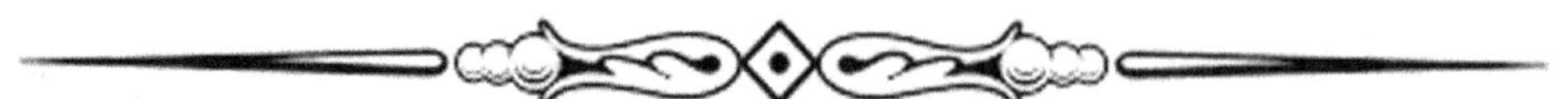

We Share

Yahweh (The God of Israel), we share in your conquering spirit.

According to Romans 8:37,

"Yet in all things we are more than conquerors

and gain an overwhelming victory through Him who loved us

[so much that He died for us]."

Verses 35-36, 38-39 assures us that nothing, not even coronavirus or other pandemics, can separate us from your love, which is in Christ Jesus our Lord. Help us to armor up in faith, put on the whole armor, and take a stand against this dread disease. Then Father, help us to share resources. If we can send money, care packs, food or aid to someone; help us to do so. Enable us to be generous and sow into the lives of others who suffer lack. If we can share encouraging words, help us to do so. Make us a care mongering people during this pandemic and beyond. Strip us of selfishness, and enable us to show compassionate for the less fortunate during this time and beyond. Give us the boldness and every resource to diligently share the good news of the Gospel with someone who is unsaved.

Colossians 3:1 says we share in His resurrection from the dead.

For that we are grateful.

In the name of Jesus, the Light of the World and One Who Sets Free. Amen.

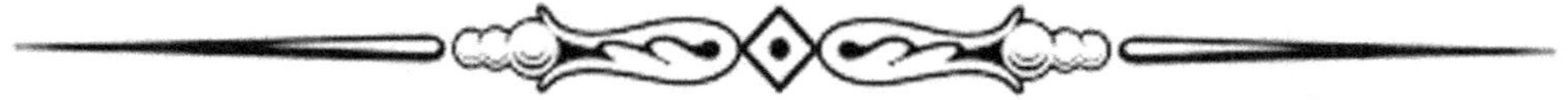

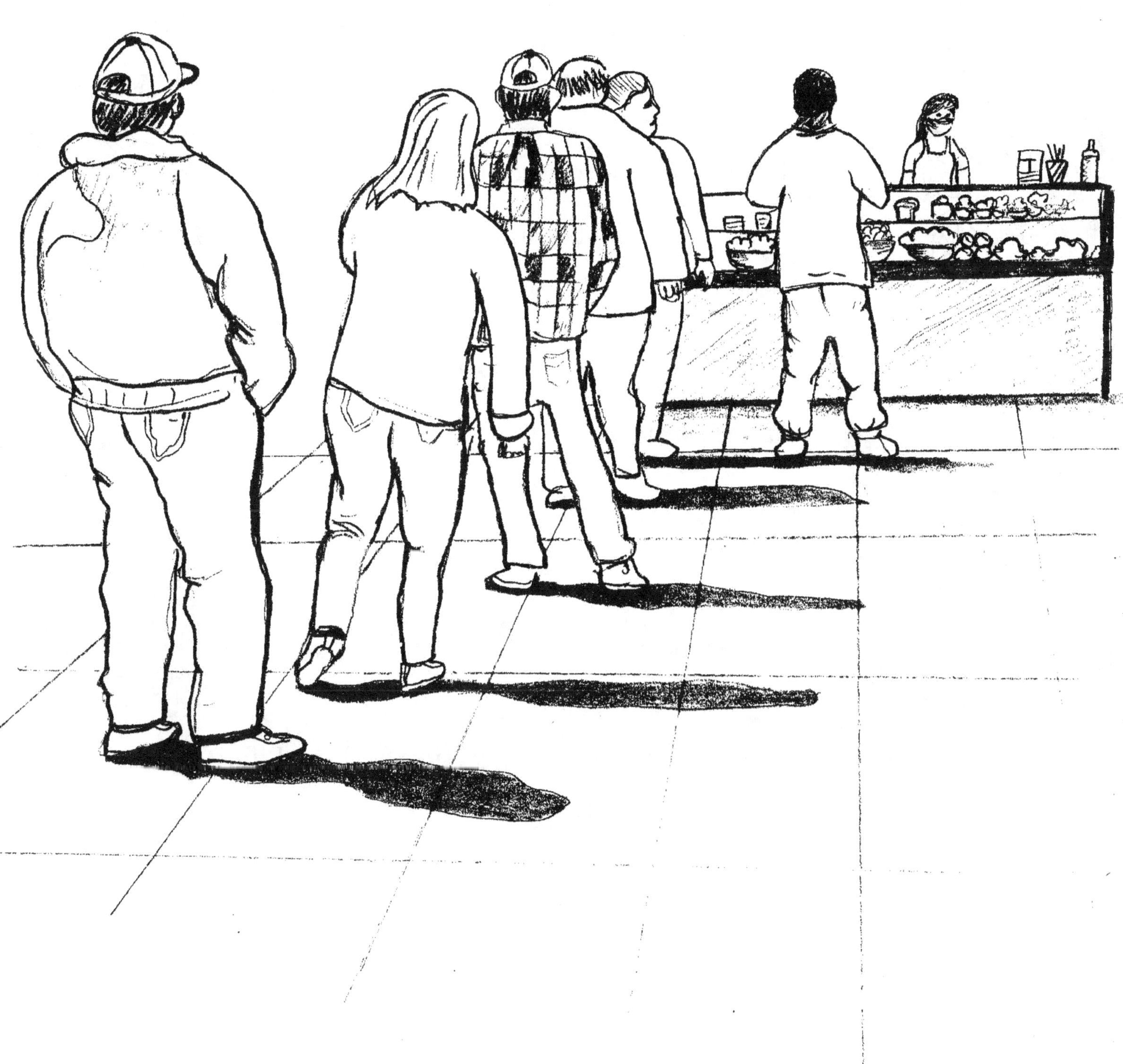

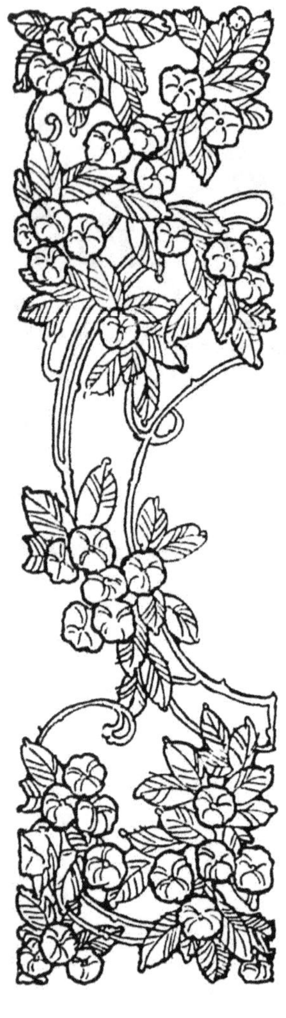

Breathe Into Us

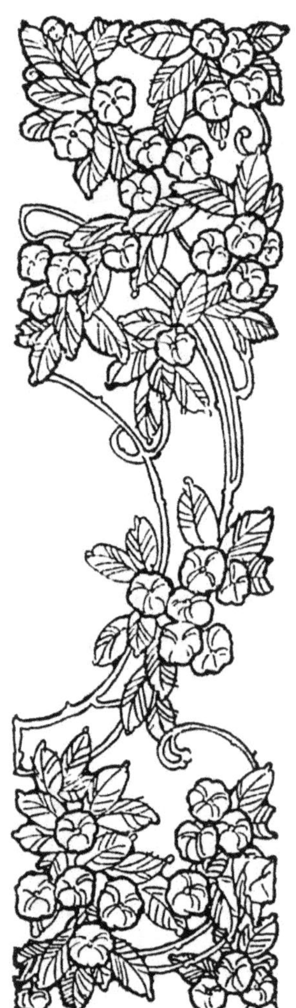

I'm asking you to be our life source,

breathe life into us –

for it is in you

in whom we live

and move

and have our being

(Acts 17:28).

In the name of Jesus, the Resurrection and the Life.

Amen.

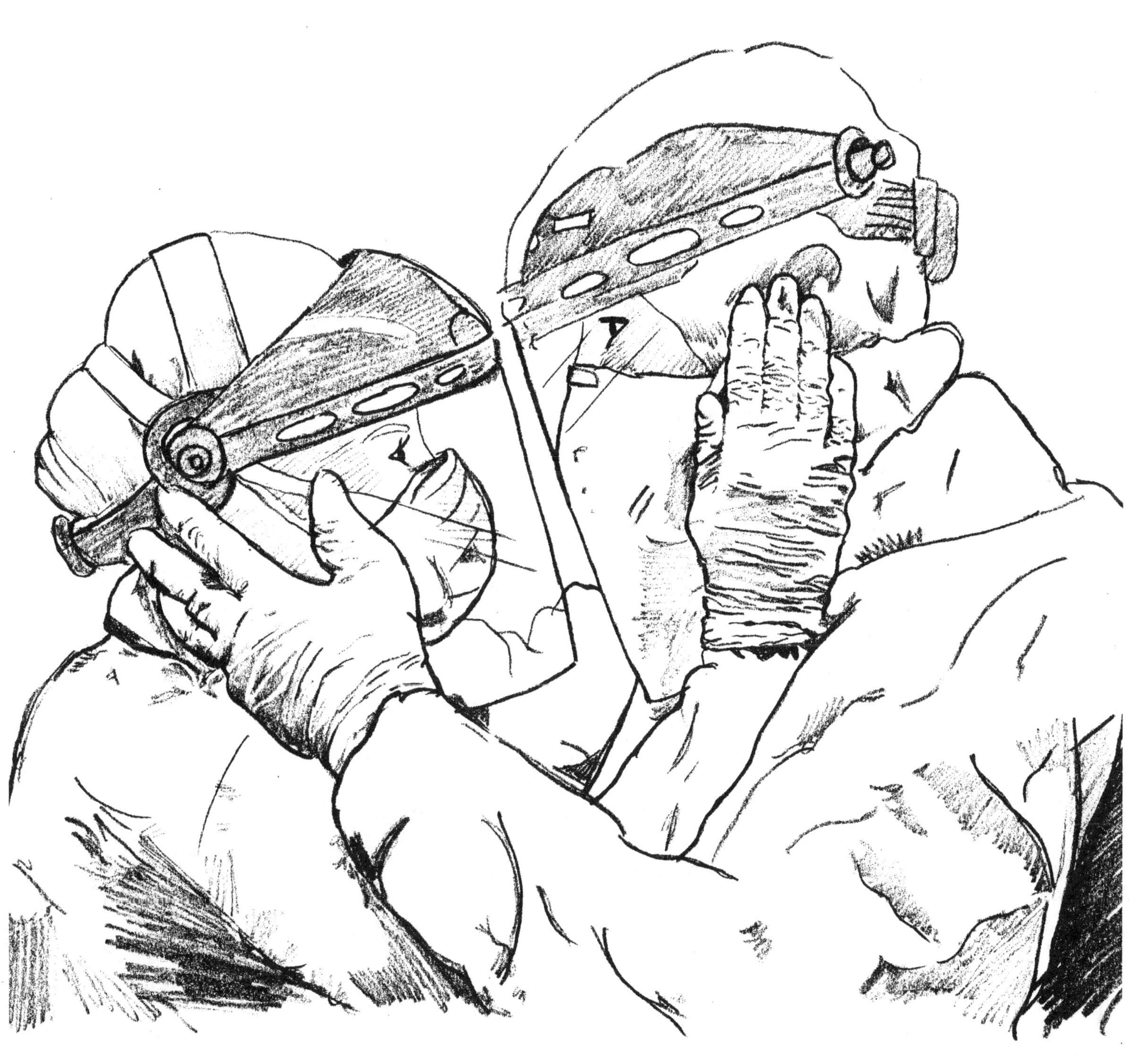

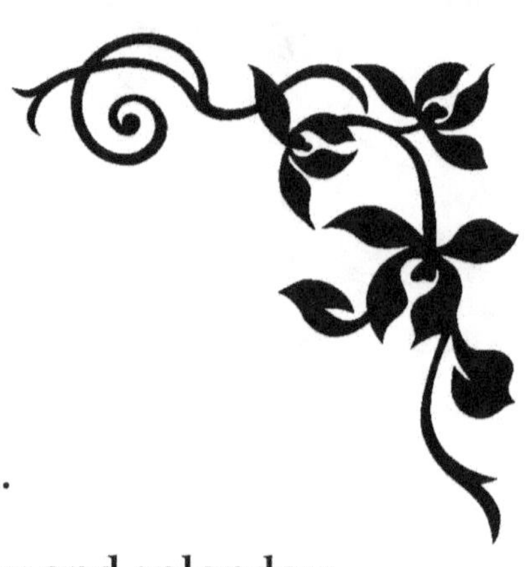

God Reigns

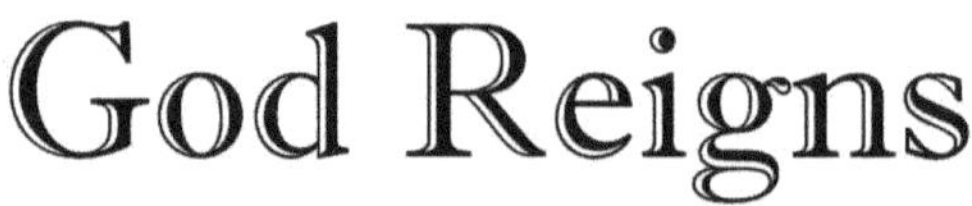

Nobody is like you, Elohim (God).

I come to you, knowing full well that you reign.

Psalm 93:1 says, "**The LORD reigns, He is clothed with majesty and splendor;**

The Lord has clothed and encircled Himself with strength;

the world is firmly established, it cannot be moved."

Lord, I come asking you to reign over my family and my life, reign over our health, and reign over this coronavirus and other pandemics, that we not experience the impact any longer. I will let you reign over my life,

for my covering and all other good things comes from you, and you alone.

When we have troubling thoughts, please **reign over our minds.**

When we have difficulty sleeping, **reign over our bedrooms and beds.**

When we have sorrow and sadness, **reign over our hearts.**

When we have financial loss and financial decreases, **reign over our finances.**

When payments are deferred but not waived,

reign over our budgets and our budget processes.

Reign over all areas of our lives –

for we are helpless and hopeless without you.

We set our hopes on you, the only one who can save both body and soul.I'm asking you to bring us into obedience to you, and your kingdom system-

that we might live, recover and be restored. In the name of Jesus, the True Vine.

Amen.

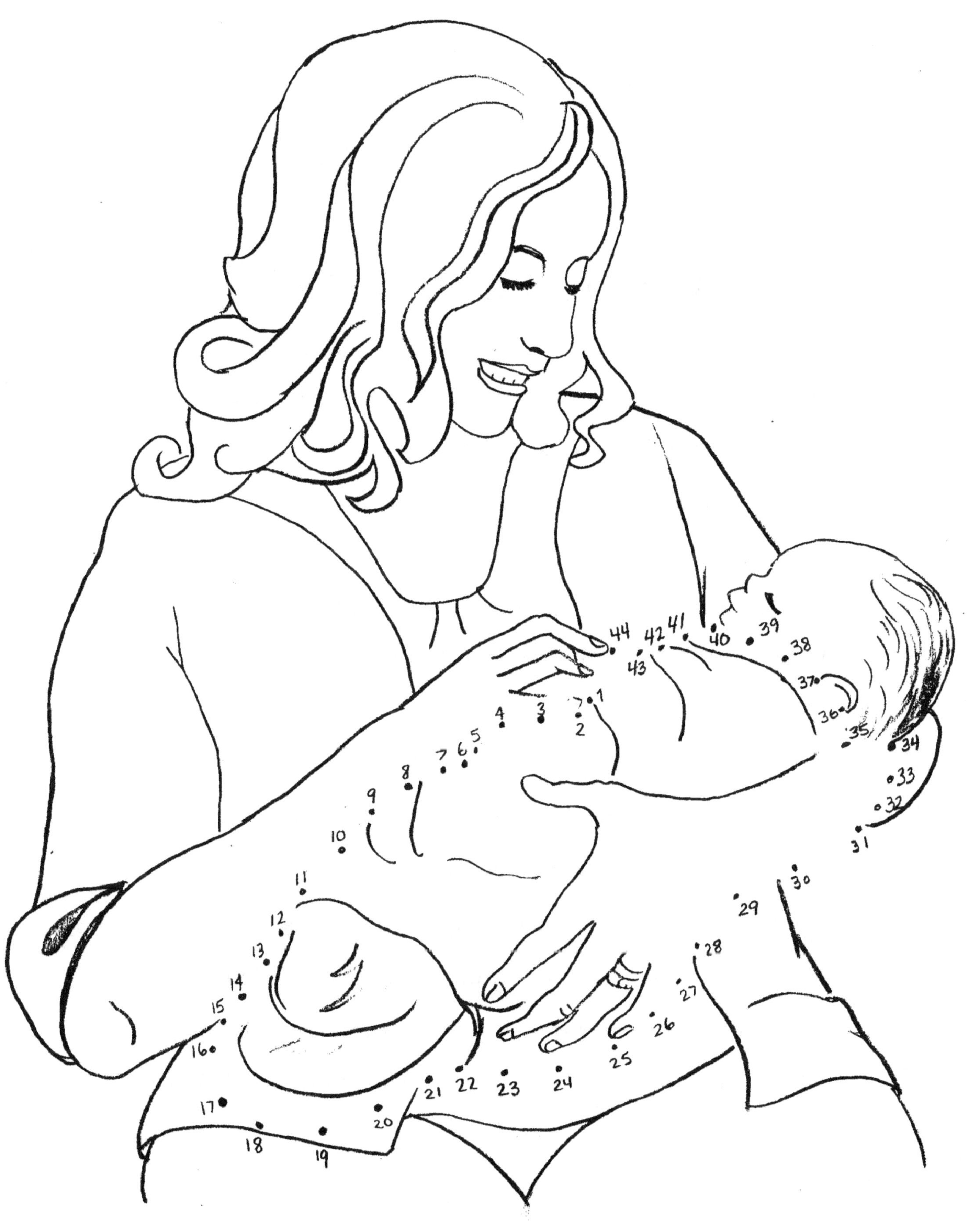

Controlling, Cohesive Force

Adonai (God), I come to you with awe-filled respect for your everlasting existence, power, might and forces for good. Colossians 1:17 declares that,

"And He Himself existed and is before all things,
and in Him all things hold together
[He is the controlling, cohesive force of the universe]."

We are a world that has external and internal foundation problems.
We call upon you, to vanquish pandemics like the coronavirus, restore us, and put us back together again.
We have turned our eyes upon you, knowing that our help comes from you.

We need you now and always.

We recognize that, and ask you for help. Help us to really see and know you from this day forward, for you alone are God.
On our knees, we surrender ourselves and cry out to you.
In the name of Jesus, The Door and Savior of the World. Amen.

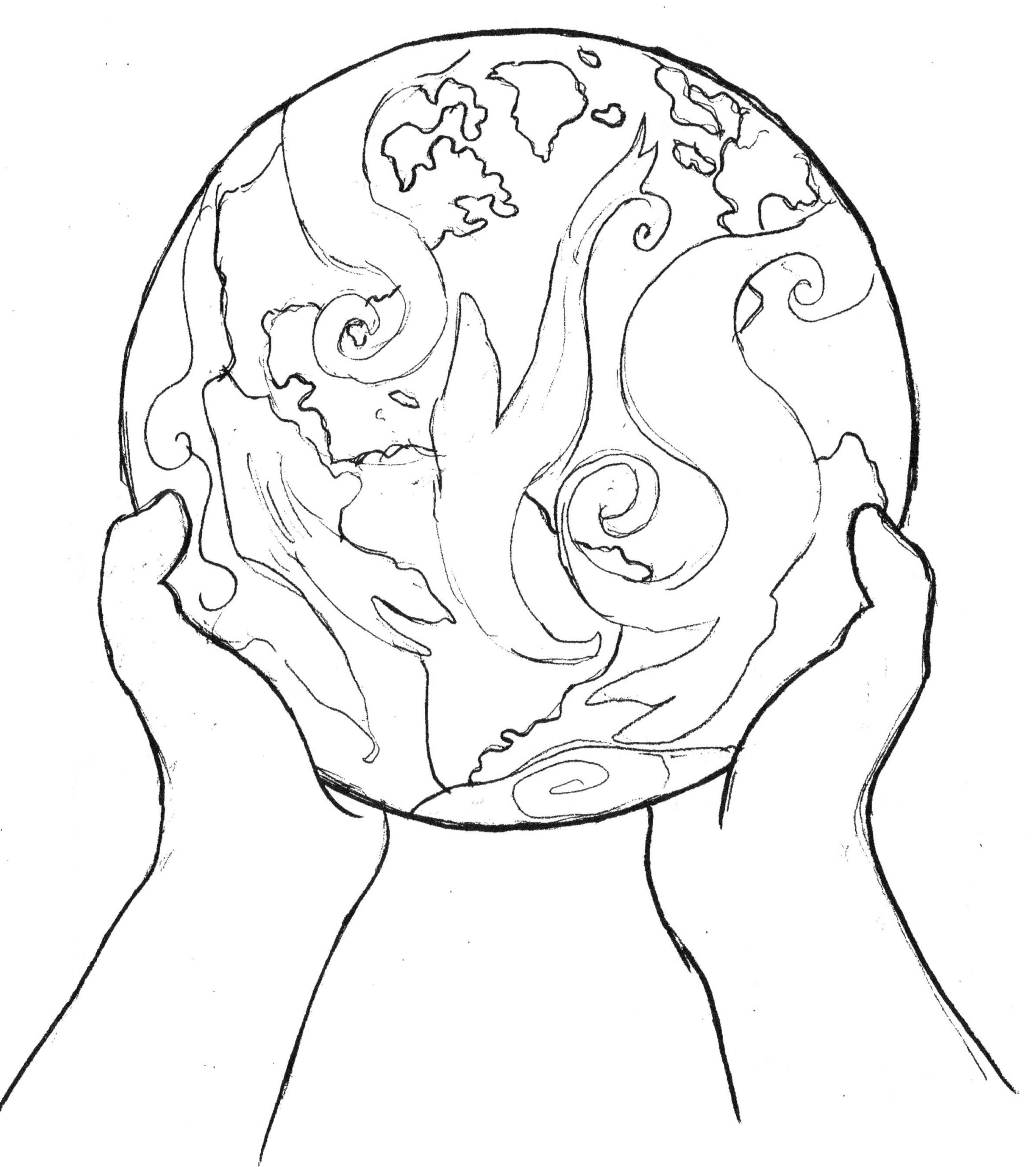

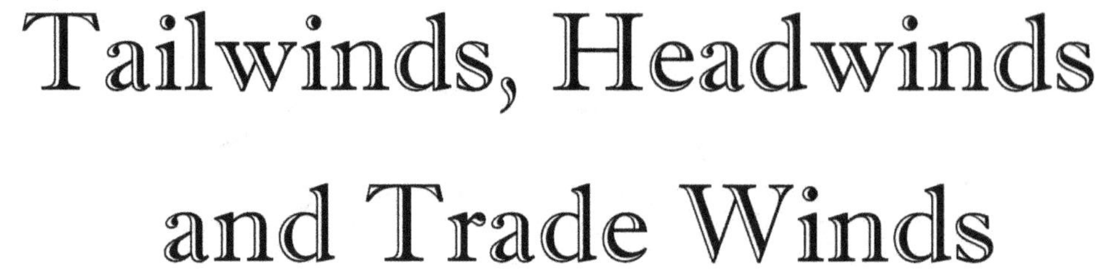

Tailwinds, Headwinds and Trade Winds

Faithful Father,

I thank you that you control the winds,

according to Mark 4:41b, where it reads,

"Who then is this, that even the wind and sea obey Him?"

We know that you control the winds, waves and that you have unlimited power. You know that tailwind of coronavirus has tried to blow our way and push us into depression, anxiety, fear, doubt, disbelief and unsound thoughts.

I'm asking you to send a headwind to block and send this virus and other pandemics back to where they came, and to make us whole and complete from this mega virus onslaught.

I'm asking you to vanquish these contagions with heavenly headwinds.

Encircle the earth, your creation, with healing, health, restoration, comfort, all kinds of provisions and your divine presence as we recover with our eyes fully turned toward you.

In the name of Jesus, Our Eternal Hope.

Amen.

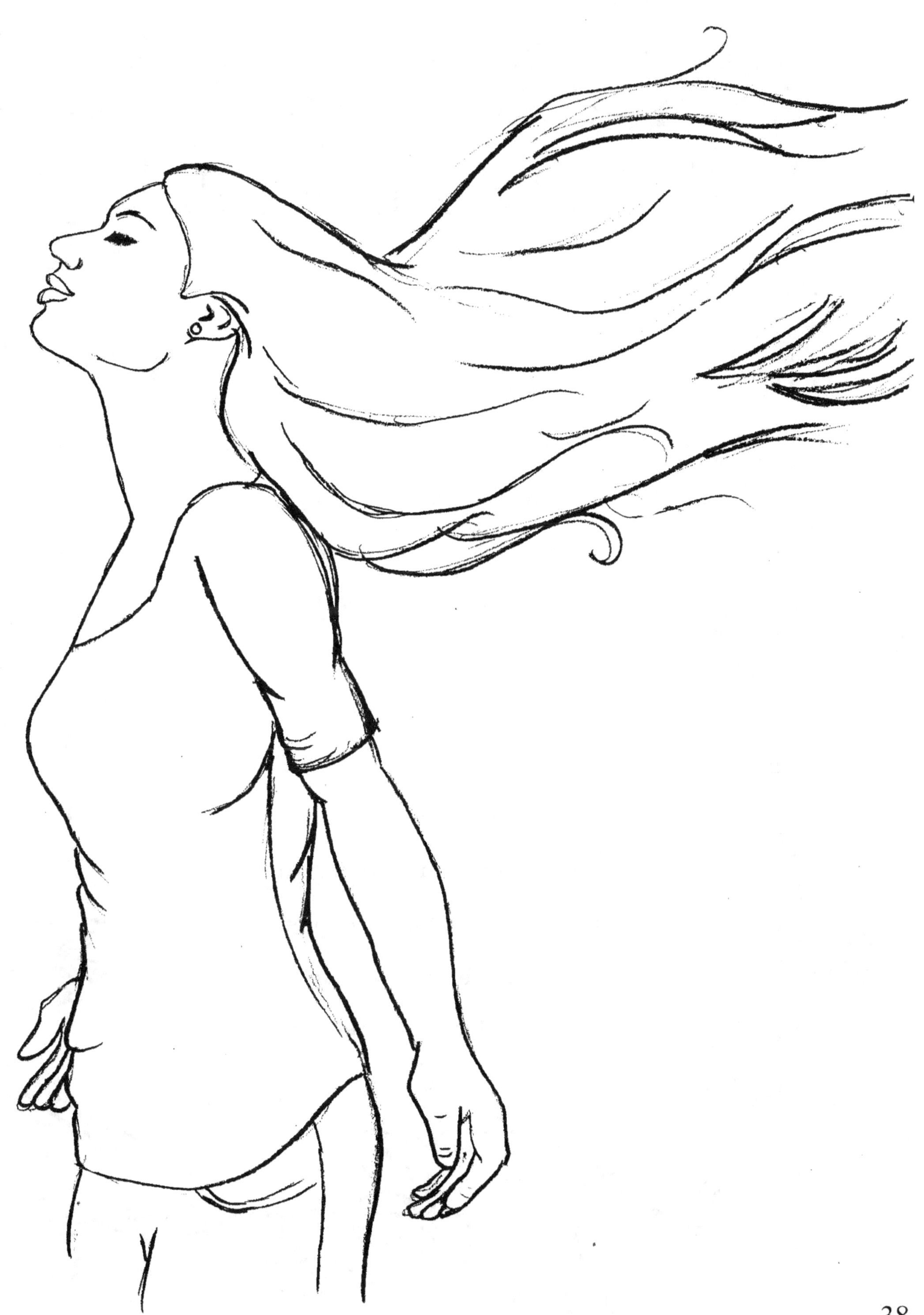

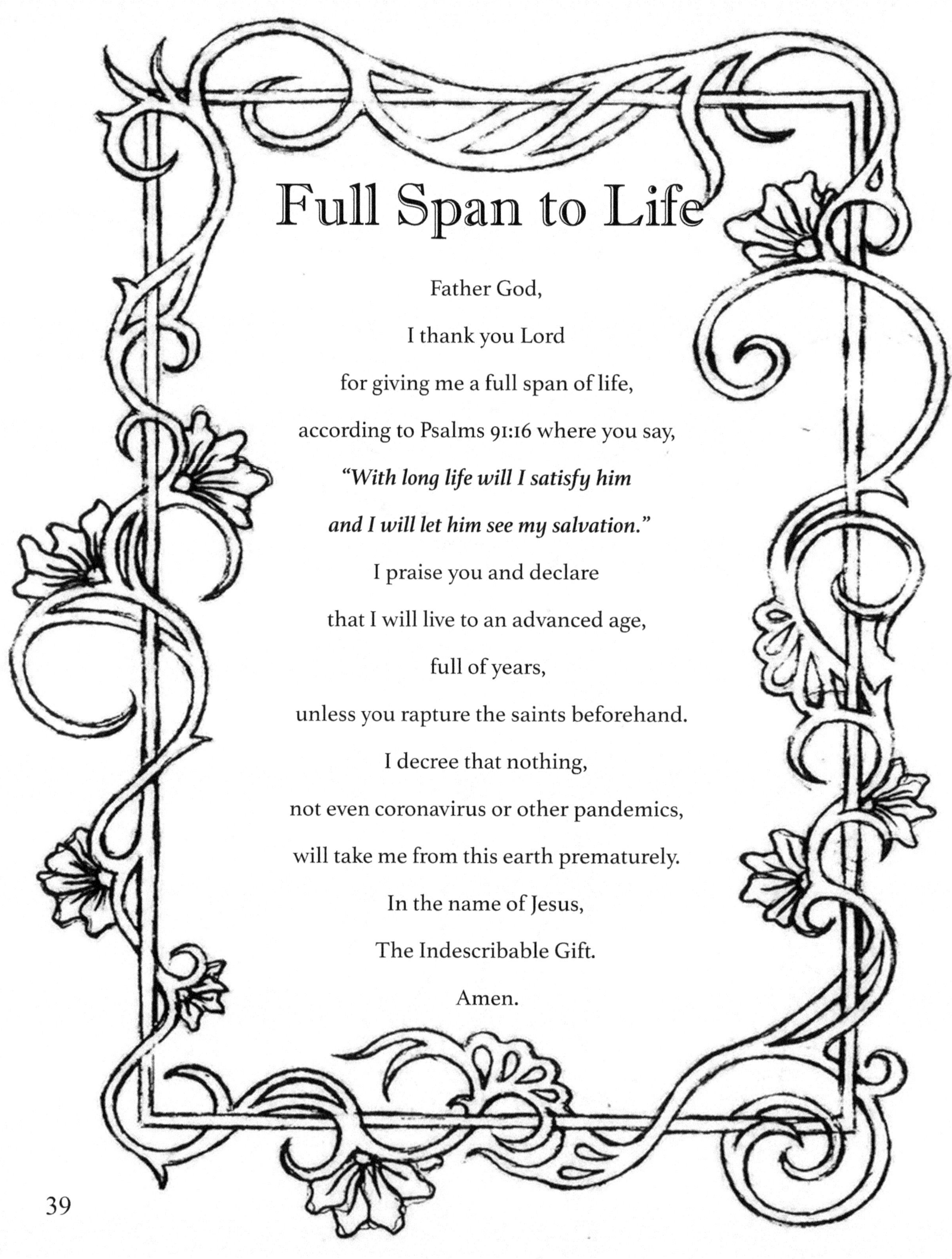

Full Span to Life

Father God,

I thank you Lord

for giving me a full span of life,

according to Psalms 91:16 where you say,

"With long life will I satisfy him

and I will let him see my salvation."

I praise you and declare

that I will live to an advanced age,

full of years,

unless you rapture the saints beforehand.

I decree that nothing,

not even coronavirus or other pandemics,

will take me from this earth prematurely.

In the name of Jesus,

The Indescribable Gift.

Amen.

Use the grid to draw and design your own mask.

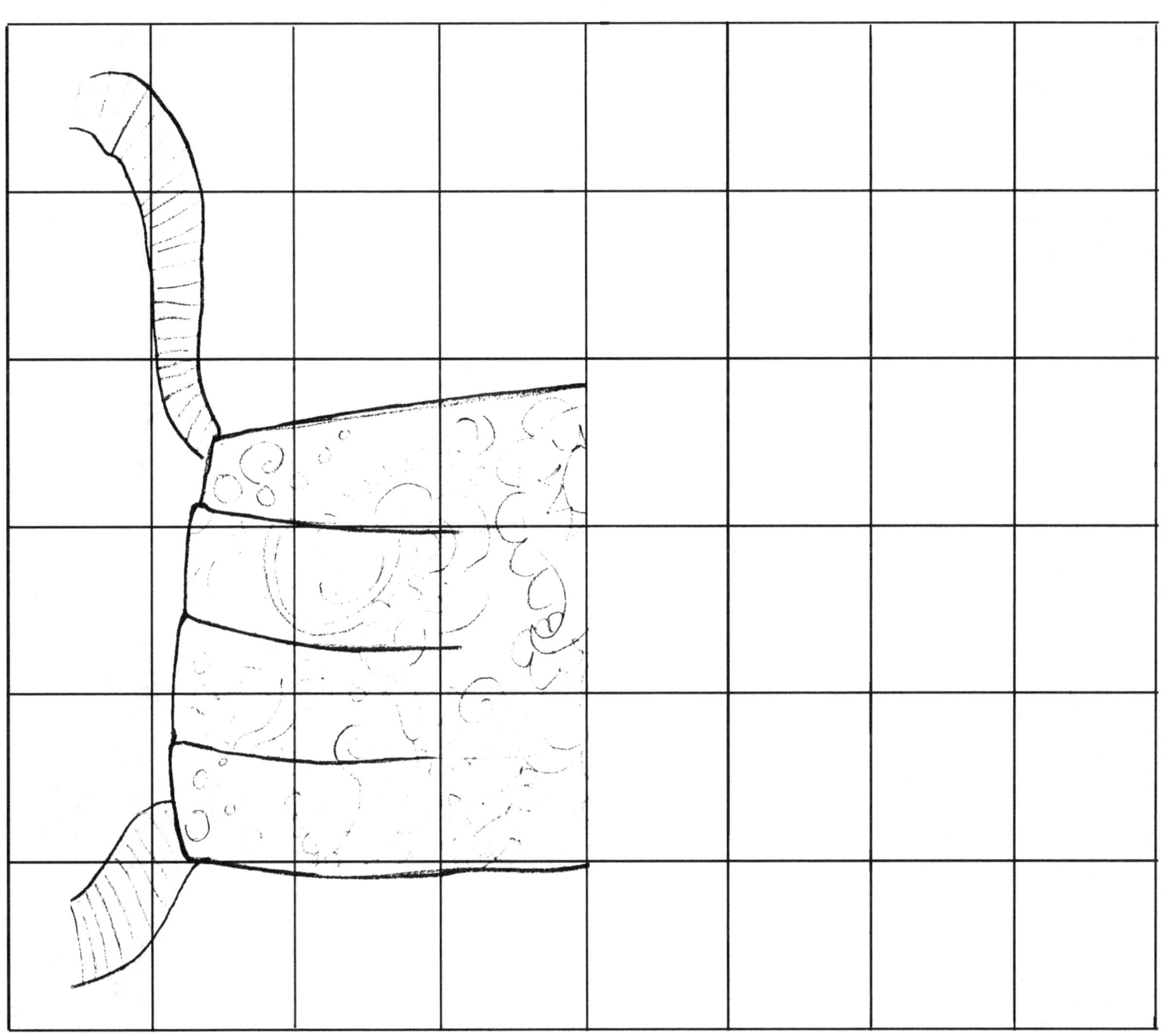

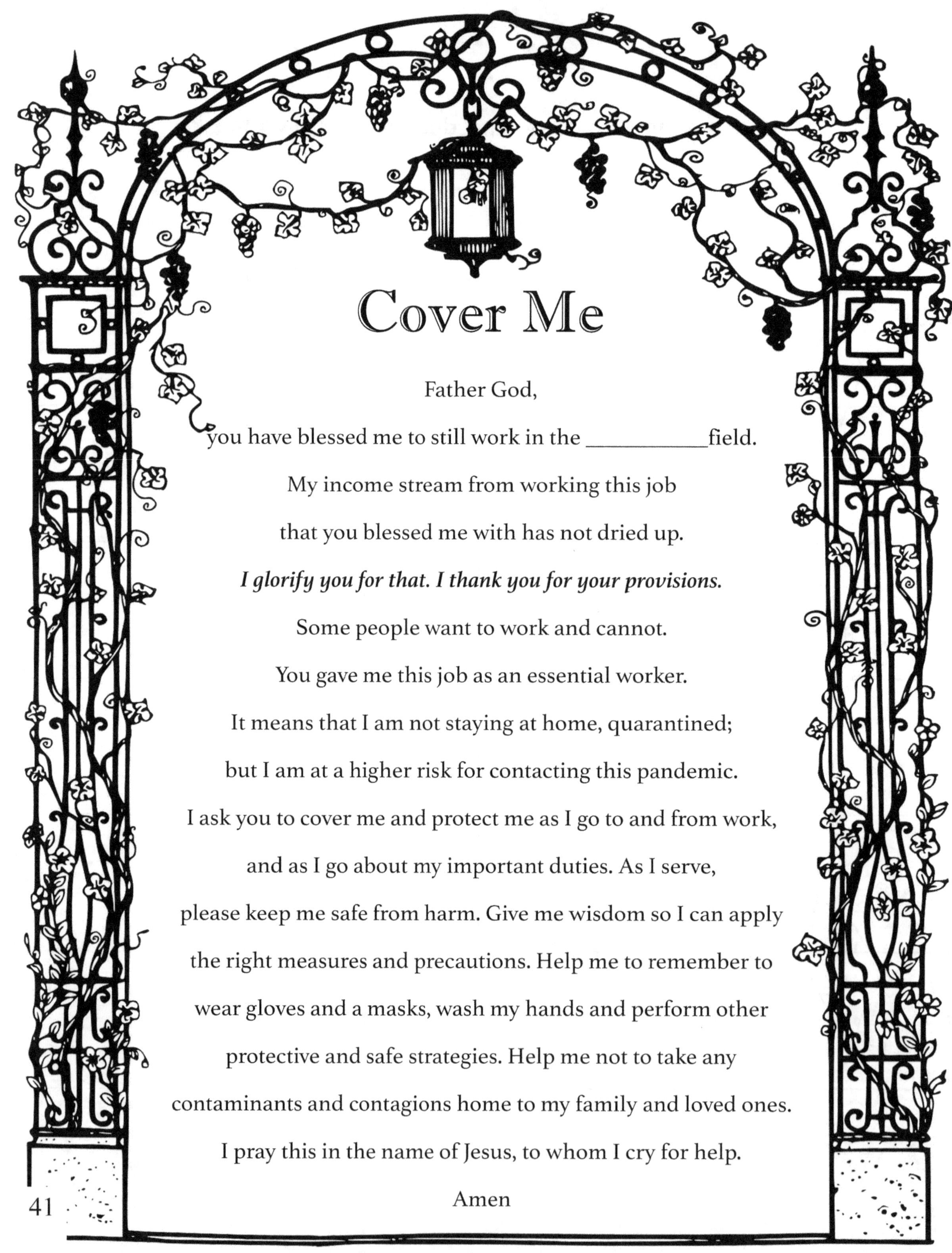

Cover Me

Father God,

you have blessed me to still work in the ___________field.

My income stream from working this job

that you blessed me with has not dried up.

I glorify you for that. I thank you for your provisions.

Some people want to work and cannot.

You gave me this job as an essential worker.

It means that I am not staying at home, quarantined;

but I am at a higher risk for contacting this pandemic.

I ask you to cover me and protect me as I go to and from work,

and as I go about my important duties. As I serve,

please keep me safe from harm. Give me wisdom so I can apply

the right measures and precautions. Help me to remember to

wear gloves and a masks, wash my hands and perform other

protective and safe strategies. Help me not to take any

contaminants and contagions home to my family and loved ones.

I pray this in the name of Jesus, to whom I cry for help.

Amen

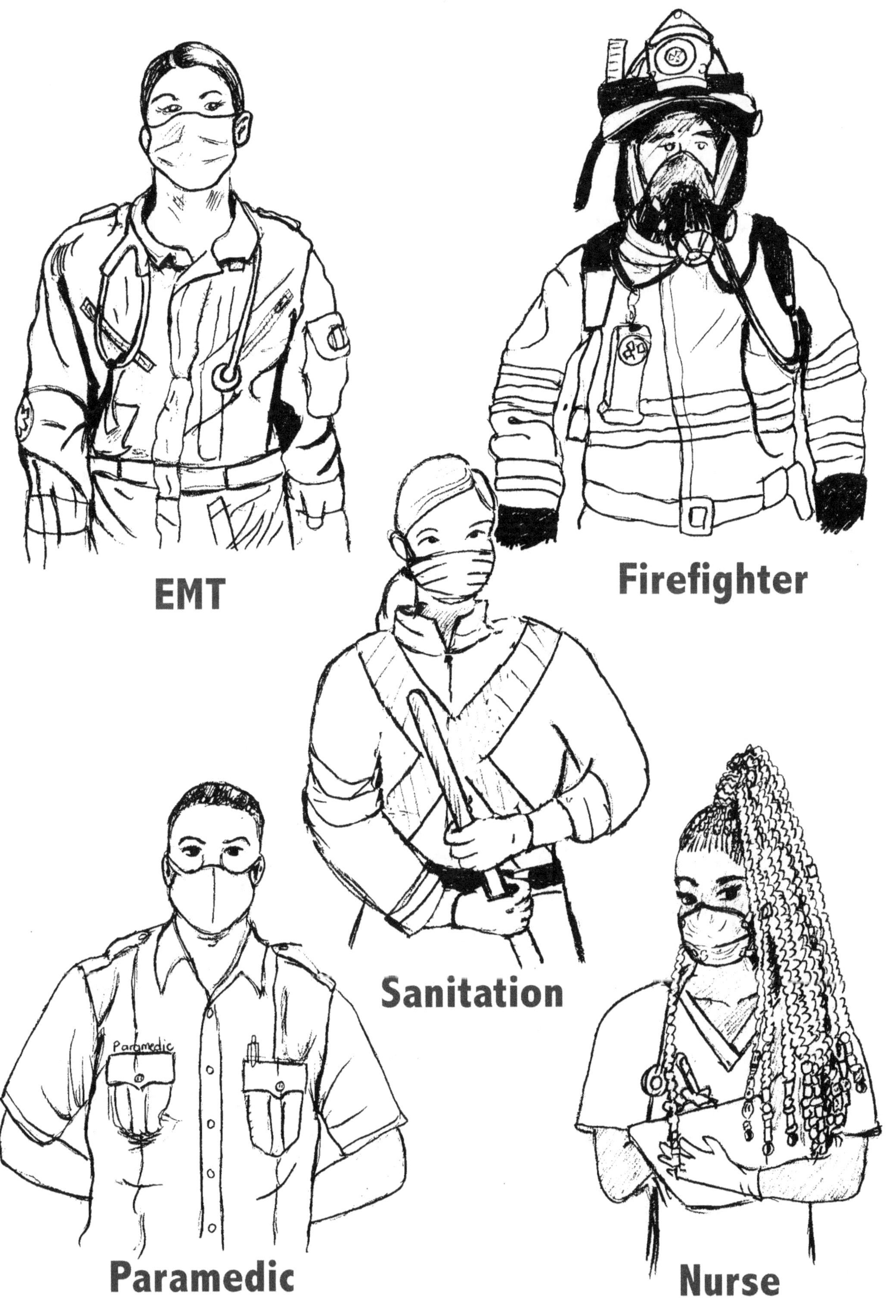
EMT
Firefighter
Sanitation
Paramedic
Paramedic
Nurse

I receive these utterances and prayers over my life, in Jesus' name.

I affix my signature as my commitment to stand in agreement.

In Jesus' name. Amen.

Signature: ________________________________

Date: ____________________________________

www.ingramcontent.com/pod-product-compliance
Lightning Source LLC
LaVergne TN
LVHW061257100826
845148LV00008B/1163

* 9 7 8 0 9 7 7 8 5 2 0 2 4 *